**Personal and Secret Message
from Premier Stalin
to the President, Mr. Roosevelt**

We have begun the offensive operations in the Stalingrad area—in its southern and northwestern sectors. The objective of the first stage is to seize the Stalingrad-Likhaya railway and disrupt the communications of the Stalingrad group of the German troops...

November 20, 1942

F. Roosevelt to J.V. Stalin

I want you to know that we have hit the Japs very hard in the Solomons. There is a probability that we have broken the backbone of the strength of their fleet, although they still have too many aircraft carriers to suit me... I am hopeful that we are going to drive the Germans out of Africa soon, and then we will give the Italians a taste of some real bombing, and I am quite sure they will never stand up to that kind of pressure.

The news from the Stalingrad area is most encouraging, and I send you my warmest congratulations.

November 26, 1942

THE SECRET HISTORY OF WORLD WAR II

THE ULTRA-SECRET WARTIME LETTERS AND CABLES OF ROOSEVELT, STALIN, AND CHURCHILL

BERKLEY BOOKS, NEW YORK

This Berkley book contains the complete
text of the original hardcover edition.
It has been completely reset in a typeface
designed for easy reading and was printed
from new film.

THE SECRET HISTORY OF WORLD WAR II

A Berkley Book/published by arrangement with
Richardson & Steirman, Inc.

PRINTING HISTORY
Richardson & Steirman edition published 1986
Berkley edition/June 1987

ISBN: 0-425-10045-6

A BERKLEY BOOK ® TM 757,375
Berkley Books are published by The Berkley Publishing Group,
200 Madison Avenue, New York, NY 10016.
The name "BERKLEY" and the stylized "B" with design
are trademarks belonging to Berkley Publishing Corporation.

PRINTED IN THE UNITED STATES OF AMERICA

EDITOR'S FOREWORD

Although Hitler had begun to devour Europe in the late 1930's, World War II officially began when Britain and France declared war on Germany on September 3, 1939, two days after Germany invaded Poland.

The Soviet Union was plunged into the war in June 1941 when 3 million German troops invaded the Soviet Union and captured Minsk, Smolensk and entered the Ukraine.

The United States declared war on Japan and Germany on December 7, 1941 after being attacked at Pearl Harbor.

Thus the British, the Russians and Americans became the Allies, united in the common battle against the Axis powers of Germany, Italy and Japan. Three great war-time leaders, Winston Churchill, Joseph Stalin and Franklin D. Roosevelt formed a bond of friendship that would last until F.D.R.'s death.

During that period of time, there was an exchange of ultra secret letters, cables and correspondence, some of which have been published. However, the previous missing link in the correspondence has been Joseph Stalin.

Now for the first time most of Stalin's letters and cables both in answer to communications from Roosevelt and Churchill, and those initiated by Stalin and are contained in this book for the first time.

The correspondence begins in 1945 and ends with Stalin's letter to President Harry Truman who succeeded Roosevelt:

FOR PRESIDENT TRUMAN

On behalf of the Soviet Government and on my own behalf, I express to the Government of the United States of America deep regret at the untimely death of Franklin Roosevelt. The American people and the United Nations have lost in the person of Franklin Roosevelt, a great statesman of world stature and a champion of post-war peace and security.

The Government of the Soviet Union expresses its heartfelt sympathy for the American people in their grievous loss and its confidence that the cooperation between the Great Powers who have borne the brunt of the war against the common foe will be promoted in the future as well.

J. Stalin

Despite this message, the seeds of the Cold War had already been sown. It began with a heated correspondence over whether the Polish Government in Exile, backed by Roosevelt and Churchill, or the Provisional Government, backed by Stalin, should be recognized. Stalin won. Then other nations in Eastern Europe began to establish communist governments.

In 1948, Churchill delivered his famous "Iron Curtain" speech in Fulton, Missouri, saying out loud what everyone knew. The Cold War had started. It wouldn't begin to thaw out until the 1970's.

But there was a period of four years, the war years, when the major powers united in a single endeavor—to defeat the common foe. It's a moment in history to remember and cherish.

As a teen-ager I served as a U.S. infantryman in Italy during 1944 and 1945. The most asked question in early 1945 was; "How far are the Russians from Berlin?" We all had the idea that when Berlin fell the war in Europe would be over and the better were our chances of surviving the war.

I was only a private. Reading and editing this book gives me a profound sense of admiration and sadness. These were the men who ran the war and were the architects of victory. And in this book we see them making momentous decisions which took months, even years to implement.

It was a memorable time in history. And it's all preserved in this volume just as it happened.

Stewart Richardson

THE SECRET
HISTORY
OF WORLD
WAR II

PART I

1941

Received on July 8, 1941

Personal Message from Mr. Churchill to Monsieur Stalin

We are all very glad here that the Russian armies are making such strong and spirited resistance to the utterly unprovoked and merciless invasion of the Nazis. There is general admiration for the bravery and tenacity of the Soviet soldiers and people. We shall do everything to help you that time, geography, and our growing resources allow. The longer the war lasts, the more help we can give. We are making very heavy attacks both by day and night with our Air Force upon all German-occupied territories and all Germany within our reach. About 400 aeroplanes made daylight sorties overseas yesterday. On Saturday night over 200 heavy bombers attacked German towns, some carrying three tons apiece, and last night nearly 250 heavy bombers were operating. This will go on. Thus we hope to force Hitler to bring back some of his air power to the West and gradually take some of the strain off you. Besides this, the Admiralty have at my desire prepared a serious operation to come off in the near future in the Arctic,

3

after which I hope that contact will be established between the British and Russian Navies. Meanwhile, by sweeping along the Norwegian coast, we have intercepted various supply ships which were moving north against you.

We welcome the arrival of the Russian Military Mission in order to concert future plans.

We have only got to go on fighting to beat the life out of the villains.

Received on July 10, 1941

Prime Minister Churchill to M. Stalin (Highly Confidential)

Ambassador Cripps, having reported his talk with you and having stated the terms of a proposed Anglo-Russian agreed declaration under two heads, namely,

(1) mutual help without any precision as to quantity or quality, and

(2) neither country to conclude a separate peace,

I have immediately convened the War Cabinet, including Mr. Fraser, Prime Minister of the Dominion of New Zealand, who is with us now. It will be necessary for us to consult with the Dominions of Canada, Australia, and South Africa, but in the meanwhile I should like to assure you that we are wholly in favor of the agreed declaration you propose. We think it should be signed as soon as we have heard from the Dominions, and published to the world immediately thereafter.

Personal Message from Stalin to Mr. Churchill

Allow me to thank you for your two personal messages.

Your messages have initiated agreement between our two Governments. Now, as you with every justification put it, the Soviet Union and Great Britain have become fighting Allies in the struggle against Hitler Germany. I have no doubt that our two countries are strong enough to defeat our common enemy in the face of all difficulties.

It may not be out of place to inform you that the position of the Soviet troops at the front remains strained. The results of Hitler's unexpected violation of the Non-Aggression Pact and the sudden attack on the Soviet Union, which have placed the German troops at an advantage, are still affecting the position of the Soviet armies. It is quite obvious that the German forces would have been far more advantageously placed if the Soviet troops had had to counter the blow, not along the line to Kishinev-Lvov-Brest-Bialystok-Kaunas and Vyborg, but along the line Odessa-Kamenets Podolsk-Minsk and the vicinity of Leningrad.

It seems to me, furthermore, that the military position of the Soviet Union, and by the same token, that of Great Britain, would improve substantially if a front were established against Hitler in the West (northern France) and the North (the Arctic).

A front in the north of France, besides diverting Hitler's forces from the East, would make impossible invasion of Britain by Hitler. Establishment of this front would be popular both with the British Army and with the population of Southern England. I am aware of the difficulty of establishing such a front, but it seems to me that, notwithstanding the difficulties, it should be done, not only for the sake of our common cause, but also in Britain's own interest. The best time to open this front is now, seeing that Hitler's forces have been switched to the East and that he has not yet been able to consolidate the positions he has taken in the East.

It would be easier still to open a front in the North. This would call for action only by British naval and air forces, without landing troops or artillery. Soviet land, naval and air forces could take part in the operation. We would be glad if Great Britain could send thither, say, one light division or more of Norwegian volunteers, who could be moved to northern Norway for insurgent operations against the Germans.

JULY 18, 1941

Message from Premier Stalin to Prime Minister Churchill

I have received your message of July 18.

I gather from the message, first, that the British Government refuses to go on supplying the Soviet Union with war materials by the northern route and, secondly, that despite the agreed Anglo-Soviet Communiqué on the adoption of urgent measures to open a second front in 1942, the British Government is putting off the operation till 1943.

According to our naval experts, the arguments of British

naval experts on the necessity of stopping delivery of war supplies to the northern harbors of the U.S.S.R. are untenable. They are convinced that, given goodwill and readiness to honor obligations, steady deliveries could be effected, with heavy loss to the Germans. The British Admiralty's order to the P.Q. 17 convoy to abandon the supply ships and return to Britain, and to the supply ships to disperse and make for Soviet harbors singly, without escort, is, in the view of our experts, puzzling and inexplicable. Of course, I do not think steady deliveries to northern Soviet ports are possible without risk or loss. But then, no major task can be carried out in wartime without risk or losses. You know, of course, that the Soviet Union is suffering far greater losses. Be that as it may, I never imagined that the British Government would deny us delivery of war materials precisely now, when the Soviet Union is badly in need of them in view of the grave situation on the Soviet-German front. It should be obvious that deliveries via Persian ports can in no way make up for the loss in the event of deliveries via the northern route being discontinued.

As to the second point, namely, that of opening a second front in Europe, I fear the matter is taking an improper turn. In view of the situation on the Soviet-German front, I state most emphatically that the Soviet Government cannot tolerate the second front in Europe being postponed till 1943.

I hope you will not take it amiss that I have seen fit to give you my frank and honest opinion and that of my colleagues on the points raised in your message.

J. STALIN

W. Churchill to J. V. Stalin
Aide-Mémoire
(Most Secret)

In reply to Premier Stalin's Aide-Mémoire of August 13th the Prime Minister of Great Britain states:

1. The best second front in 1942, and the only large-scale operation possible from the Atlantic, is "Torch." If this can be effected in October, it will give more aid to Russia than any other plan. It also prepares the way for 1943 and has the four advantages mentioned by Premier Stalin in the conversation of August 12th. The British and United States Governments have made up their minds about this and all preparations are proceeding with the utmost speed.

2. Compared with "Torch," the attack with 6 or 8 Anglo-American Divisions on the Cherbourg Peninsula and the Channel Islands would be a hazardous and futile operation. The Germans have enough troops in the West to block us in this narrow peninsula with fortified lines, and would concentrate all their air forces in the West upon it. In the opinion of all the British Naval, Military, and Air authorities, the operation could only end in disaster. Even if the lodgment were made, it would not bring a single division back from Russia. It would also be far more a running sore for us than for the enemy, and would use up wastefully and wantonly the key men and the landing craft required for real action in 1943. This is our settled view. The Chief of the Imperial General Staff will go into details with the Russian Commanders to any extent that may be desired.

3. No promise has been broken by Great Britain or the

United States. I point to paragraph 5 of my Aide-Mémoire given to Mr. Molotov on the 10th June, 1942, which distinctly says: "We can, therefore, give no promise." This Aide-Mémoire followed upon lengthy conversations, in which the very small chance of such a plan being adopted was made abundantly clear. Several of these conversations are on record.

4. However, all the talk about an Anglo-American invasion of France this year has misled the enemy, and has held large air forces and considerable military forces on the French Channel coast. It would be injurious to all common interests, especially Russian interests, if any public controversy arose in which it would be necessary for the British Government to unfold to the nation the crushing argument which they conceive themselves to possess against "Sledgehammer." Widespread discouragement would be caused to the Russian armies who have been buoyed up on this subject, and the enemy would be free to withdraw further forces from the West. The wisest course is to use "Sledgehammer" as a blind for "Torch," and proclaim "Torch," when it begins, as the second front. This is what we ourselves mean to do.

5. We cannot admit that the conversations with Mr. Molotov about the second front, safeguarded as they were by reservations both oral and written, formed any ground for altering the strategic plans of the Russian High Command.

6. We reaffirm our resolve to aid our Russian allies by every practicable means.

W. CH.

A U G U S T   1 4 ,   1 9 4 2

Received on August 15, 1941

F. Roosevelt and W. Churchill to J. V. Stalin

We have taken the opportunity afforded by the consideration of the report of Mr. Harry Hopkins on his return from Moscow to consult together as to how best our two countries can help your country in the splendid defense that you are putting up against the Nazi attack. We are at the moment cooperating to provide you with the very maximum of supplies that you most urgently need. Already many shiploads have left our shores and more will leave in the immediate future.

We must now turn our minds to the consideration of a more long-term policy, since there is still a long and hard path to be traversed before there can be won that complete victory without which our efforts and sacrifices would be wasted.

The war goes on upon many fronts, and before it is over, there may be yet further fighting fronts that will be developed. Our resources, though immense, are limited, and it must become a question of where and when those resources can best be used to further our common effort to the greatest extent. This applies equally to manufactured war supplies and to raw materials.

The needs and demands of your and our armed services can only be determined in the light of the full knowledge of the many facts which must be taken into consideration in the decisions that we take. In order that all of us may be in a position to arrive at speedy decisions as to the apportionment of our joint resources, we suggest that we prepare a meeting which should be held at Moscow, to which we would send high representatives who could discuss these matters directly with you. If this conference appeals to you, we want you to know that pending the decisions of that conference we shall continue to send supplies and material as rapidly as possible.

We realize fully how vitally important to the defeat of Hitlerism is the brave and steadfast resistance of the Soviet Union, and we feel therefore that we must not in any circumstances fail to act quickly and immediately in this matter of planning the program for the future allocation of our joint resources.

> *Franklin D. ROOSEVELT*
> *Winston S. CHURCHILL*

Received on August 30, 1941

Personal Message
from Prime Minister Churchill
to Monsieur Stalin

I have been searching for any way to give you help in your splendid resistance pending the long-term arrangements which we are discussing with the United States of America and which will form the subject of the Moscow Conference. M. Maisky has represented that fighter aircraft are much needed in view of your heavy losses. We are expediting the dispatch of the 200 Tomahawks about which I telegraphed in my last message. Our two squadrons should reach Murmansk about September 6th, comprising 40 Hurricanes. You will, I am sure, realize that fighter aircraft are the foundation of our home defense, besides which we are trying to obtain air superiority in Libya and also to provide Turkey so as to bring her in on our side. Nevertheless I could send 200 more Hurricanes, making 440 fighters in all, if your pilots could use them effectively. These would be eight- and twelve-gun Hurricanes, which we have found very deadly in action. We could send 100 now and two batches of fifty soon afterwards, together with mechanics, instructors, spare parts and equipment, to Archangel. Meanwhile, arrangements could be made to begin accustoming your pilots and mechanics to the new type if you send them to our squadrons at Murmansk. If you feel that this would be useful, orders will be given here accordingly, and a full technical memorandum is being telegraphed through our Military Air Mission.

The news that the Persians have decided to cease resistance is most welcome. Even more than safeguarding the oil fields, our object in entering Persia has been to get another through route to you which cannot be cut. For this purpose we must develop the railway from the Persian Gulf to the Caspian and make sure that it runs smoothly with reinforcements of railway material from India. The Foreign Secretary has given to M. Maisky for you the kind of terms which we should like to make with the Persian Government so as to have a friendly people and not be compelled to waste a number of divisions merely guarding the railway line. Food is being sent from India, and if the Persians submit, we shall resume the payment of oil royalties now due to the Shah. We are instructing our advance guards to push on and join hands with your forces at a point to be fixed by the military commanders somewhere between Hamadan and Qazvin. It would be a good thing to let the world know that the British and Soviet forces had actually joined hands. In our view it would be better at this moment for neither of us to enter Tehran in force, as all we want is a through route. We are making a large-scale base at Basra, and we hope to make this a well-equipped warm-water reception port for American supplies, which can thus surely reach the Caspian and Volga regions.

I must again express the admiration of the British nation

for the wonderful fight which the Russian armies and the Russian people are making against the Nazi criminals. General MacFarlane was immensely impressed by all he saw at the front. A very hard time lies before us, but Hitler will not have a pleasant winter under our ever-increasing air bombardment. I was gratified by the very firm warning which Your Excellency gave to Japan about supplies via Vladivostok. President Roosevelt seemed disposed, when I met him, to take a strong line against further Japanese aggression, whether in the South or in the Northwest Pacific, and I made haste to declare that we would range ourselves upon his side should war come. I am most anxious to do more for General Chiang Kai-shek than we have hitherto felt strong enough to do. We do not want war with Japan, and I am sure that the way to stop it is to confront these people, who are divided and far from sure of themselves, with the prospect of the heaviest combination.

———

Sent on September 3, 1941

Personal Message from Premier Stalin to the Prime Minister Mr. Churchill

Please accept my thanks for the promise to sell to the Soviet Union another 200 fighter aeroplanes in addition to the 200 fighters promised earlier. I have no doubt that Soviet pilots will succeed in mastering them and putting them to use.

I must say, however, that these aircraft, which it appears we shall not be able to use soon and not all at once, but at intervals and in groups, cannot seriously change the situation on the Eastern Front. They cannot do so not merely because of the scale of the war, which necessitates the continuous dispatch of large numbers of aircraft, but also, and chiefly, because during the last three weeks, the position of the Soviet troops has considerably deteriorated in such vital areas as the Ukraine and Leningrad.

The fact is that the relative stabilization of the front, achieved some three weeks ago, has been upset in recent weeks by the arrival of 30-34 fresh German infantry divisions and enormous numbers of tanks and aircraft at the Eastern Front, and also by the activization of 20 Finnish and 26 Rumanian divisions. The Germans look on the threat in the West as a bluff, so they are moving all their forces from the West to the East with impunity, knowing that there is no second front in the West nor is there likely to be one. They think it perfectly possible that they will be able to beat their enemies one at a time—first the Russians and then the British.

As a result, we have lost more than half the Ukraine and, what is more, the enemy is now at the gates of Leningrad.

These circumstances have led to our loss of the Krivoi Rog iron-ore area and a number of iron and steel works in the Ukraine, to the evacuation by us of an aluminum plant on the Dnieper and another in Tikhvin, a motor plant and two aircraft plants in the Ukraine, and two motor and two aircraft plants in Leningrad, which cannot begin production on their new sites before seven or eight months.

This has resulted in a lessening of our defense capacity and has confronted the Soviet Union with mortal danger.

Here it is pertinent to ask: what is the way out of this more than unfavorable situation?

I think the only way is to open a second front this year somewhere in the Balkans or in France, one that would divert 30-40 German divisions from the Eastern Front, and simultaneously to supply the Soviet Union with 30,000 tons of aluminum by the beginning of October and a minimum monthly aid of 400 aeroplanes and 500 tanks (of small or medium size).

Without these two kinds of aid, the Soviet Union will be either defeated or weakened to the extent that it will lose for a long time the ability to help its Allies by active operations at the front against Hitlerism.

I realize that this message will cause Your Excellency some

vexation. But that cannot be helped. Experience has taught me to face up to reality, no matter how unpleasant it may be, and not to shrink from telling the truth, no matter how unpleasant.

The matter of Iran came off well indeed. Joint operations by the British and Soviet troops settled the issue. And so it will be in the future, as long as our forces operate jointly. But Iran is merely an episode. It is not in Iran, of course, that the outcome of the war will be decided.

The Soviet Union, like Britain, does not want war with Japan. The Soviet Union does not deem it possible to violate treaties, including the treaty of neutrality with Japan. But should Japan violate that treaty and attack the Soviet Union, she will be properly rebuffed by Soviet troops.

In conclusion, allow me to thank you for the admiration you have expressed for the operations of the Soviet troops, who are waging a bloody war against Hitler's robber hordes for our common liberation cause.

His Excellency Monsieur Joseph Stalin

My dear Premier Stalin,

The British and American Missions have now started, and this letter will be presented to you by Lord Beaverbrook. Lord Beaverbrook has the fullest confidence of the Cabinet, and is one of my oldest and most intimate friends. He has established the closest relations with Mr. Harriman, who is a remarkable American, wholeheartedly devoted to the victory of the common cause. They will lay before you all that we have been able to arrange in much anxious consultation between Great Britain and the United States.

President Roosevelt has decided that our proposals shall, in the first instance, deal with the monthly quotas we shall send to you in the nine-months period from October 1941 to June 1942 inclusive. You have the right to know exactly what we can deliver month-by-month in order that you may handle your reserves to the best advantage.

The American proposals have not yet gone beyond the end of June 1942, but I have no doubt that considerably larger quotas can be furnished by both countries thereafter, and you may be sure we shall do our utmost to repair as far as possible the grievous curtailments which your war industries have suffered through the Nazi invasion. I will not anticipate what Lord Beaverbrook will have to say upon this subject.

You will realize that the quotas up to the end of June 1942 are supplied almost entirely out of British production, or production which the United States would have given us under our own purchases or under the Lease-and-Lend Bill. The United States were resolved to give us virtually the whole of their exportable surplus, and it is not easy for them within that time to open out effectively new sources of supply. I am hopeful that a further great impulse will be given to the production of the United States, and that by 1943 the mighty industry of America will be in full war swing. For our part, we shall not only make substantially increased contributions from our own existing forecast production, but also try to obtain from our people an extra further effort to meet our common needs. You will understand, however, that our Army and its supply which has been planned is perhaps only one-fifth or one-sixth as large as that of yours or Germany's. Our first duty and need is to keep open the seas, and our second duty is to obtain decisive superiority in the air. These have the first claims upon the manpower of our 44,000,000 in the British Islands. We can never hope to have an Army or Army munitions industries comparable to those of the great Continental military Powers. Nonetheless, we will do our utmost to aid you.

General Ismay, who is my personal representative on the Chiefs of the Staffs Committee, and is thoroughly acquainted with the whole field of our military policy, is authorized to study with your Commanders any plans for practical cooperation which may suggest themselves.

If we can clear our western flank in Libya of the enemy, we

shall have considerable forces, both Air and Army, to cooperate upon the southern flank of the Russian front.

It seems to me that the most speedy and effective help would come if Turkey could be induced to resist a German demand for the passage of troops, or better still, if she would enter the war on our side. You will, I am sure, attach due weight to this.

I have always shared your sympathy for the Chinese people in their struggle to defend their native land against Japanese aggression. Naturally, we do not want to add Japan to the side of our foes, but the attitude of the United States, resulting from my conference with President Roosevelt, has already enforced a far more sober view upon the Japanese Government. I made haste to declare on behalf of His Majesty's Government that should the United States be involved in war with Japan, Great Britain would immediately range herself on her side. I think that all our three countries should, so far as possible, continue to give aid to China, and that this may go to considerable lengths without provoking a Japanese declaration of war.

There is no doubt that a long period of struggle and suffering lies before our peoples, but I have great hopes that the United States will enter the war as a belligerent, and if so, I cannot doubt that we have but to endure to conquer.

I am hopeful that as the war continues, the great masses of the peoples of the British Empire, the Soviet Union, the United States, and China, which alone comprise two-thirds of the entire human race, may be found marching together against their persecutors; and I am sure the road they travel will lead to victory.

With heartfelt wishes for the success of the Russian Armies, and of the ruin of the Nazi tyrants,

Believe me,

> *Yours sincerely,*
> *Winston S. CHURCHILL*

SEPTEMBER 21, 1941

Received on September 30, 1941

F. Roosevelt to J. V. Stalin

My dear Mr. Stalin,

This note will be presented to you by my friend Averell Harriman, whom I have asked to be head of our delegation to Moscow.

Mr. Harriman is well aware of the strategic importance of your front and will, I know, do everything that he can to bring the negotiations in Moscow to a successful conclusion.

Harry Hopkins has told me in great detail of his encouraging and satisfactory visits with you. I can't tell you how thrilled all of us are because of the gallant defense of the Soviet armies.

I am confident that ways will be found to provide the material and supplies necessary to fight Hitler on all fronts, including your own.

I want particularly to take this occasion to express my great confidence that your armies will ultimately prevail over Hitler and to assure you of our great determination to be of every possible material assistance.

Yours very sincerely,
Franklin D. ROOSEVELT

J. V. Stalin to W. Churchill

My dear Prime Minister Churchill,

The arrival of the British and American Missions in Moscow, and particularly the fact that they were led by Lord Beaverbrook and Mr. Harriman, had a most favorable effect. As for Lord Beaverbrook, he did his utmost to expedite consideration and, possibly, solution of the most pressing problems discussed at the Moscow Tripartite Conference and to make them fruitful. I can say the same for Mr. Harriman. I wish therefore to convey to you and Mr. Roosevelt the sincere gratitude of the Soviet Government for sending such authoritative representatives to Moscow.

I admit that our present requirements in military supplies, arising from a number of unfavorable circumstances on our front and the resulting evacuation of a further group of enterprises, to say nothing of the fact that a number of issues have been put off until final consideration and settlement in London and Washington, transcend the decisions agreed at the conference. Nevertheless, the Moscow Conference did a great deal of important work. I hope the British and American Governments will do all they can to increase the monthly quotas and also to seize the slightest opportunity to accelerate the planned deliveries right now, since the Hitlerites will use the prewinter months to exert the utmost pressure on the U.S.S.R.

With regard to both Turkey and China, I agree with the considerations you have stated. I hope the British Government is displaying the proper activity at the moment in both directions, because this is particularly important now that the U.S.S.R.'s opportunities are naturally limited.

As regards the prospects of our common struggle against

the bandits' lair of Hitlerites, who have entrenched themselves in the heart of Europe, I am confident that despite the difficulties we shall secure the defeat of Hitler in the interest of our freedom-loving peoples.

Yours sincerely,
J. STALIN

OCTOBER 3, 1941

J. V. Stalin to F. Roosevelt

My dear Mr. Roosevelt,

Your letter has reached me through Mr. Harriman.

I avail myself of this opportunity to express to you the Soviet Government's deep gratitude for having entrusted the leadership of the U.S. delegation to such an authoritative person as Mr. Harriman, whose participation in the Moscow Three-Power Conference was so fruitful.

I have no doubt that you will do all that is necessary to ensure implementation of the Moscow Conference decisions as speedily and fully as possible, all the more because the Hitlerites will certainly try to use the pre-winter months for exerting maximum pressure upon the U.S.S.R. at the front.

Like you, I am confident of final victory over Hitler for the countries now joining their efforts to accelerate the elimination of bloody Hitlerism, a goal for which the Soviet Union is now making such big and heavy sacrifices.

Yours very sincerely,
J. STALIN

OCTOBER 3, 1941

Aide-Mémoire

Handed to A. Y. Vyshinsky by the U.S. Ambassador, Mr. Steinhardt, on November 2, 1941

In a personal message to Mr. Stalin, President Roosevelt states:

(1) That he has seen the Protocol of the Three-Power Conference in Moscow and has discussed with the members of the American Mission the data set forth therein.

(2) That he has approved all the items of military equipment and munitions and has directed that the raw materials be provided so far as possible as rapidly as possible.

(3) That he has given orders that the deliveries are to begin at once and are to be continued in the largest possible volume.

(4) So as to obviate any financial difficulties, he has directed that there be effected immediately arrangements under which shipments may be made under the Lease-Lend Act up to the value of $1,000,000,000.

(5) He proposes, subject to the approval of the Soviet Government, that no interest be charged by the United States on such indebtedness as may be incurred by the Soviet Government arising out of these shipments and that on such indebtedness as the Soviet Government may incur, payments shall begin only five years after the end of the war, and that the payments be made over a period of ten years after the expiration of this five-year period.

(6) The President hopes that the Soviet Government will make special efforts to sell such commodities and raw materials to the United States as may be available and of which the United States may be in need, the proceeds of sales to the

United States to be credited on the account of the Government of the Soviet Union.

(7) The President takes the opportunity to thank the Soviet Government for the speedy manner in which the Three-Power Conference in Moscow was conducted by Mr. Stalin and his associates and assures him that the implications of that Conference will be carried out to the utmost.

(8) The President expresses the hope that Mr. Stalin will not hesitate to communicate with him directly should the occasion require.

Kuibyshev, November 2, 1941

J. V. Stalin to F. Roosevelt

Mr. President,

I have not yet received the text of your message, but on November 2 Mr. Steinhardt, the United States Ambassador, delivered to me through Mr. Vyshinsky an Aide-Mémoire giving its substance.

I should like first of all to express complete agreement with your appraisal of the results of the Three-Power Conference in Moscow, which should be credited primarily to Mr. Harriman and to Mr. Beaverbrook who did their best to bring the Conference to an early and successful conclusion. The Soviet Government is most grateful for your statement that the implications of the Conference will be carried out to the utmost.

Your decision, Mr. President, to grant the Soviet Union an interest-free loan to the value of $1,000,000,000 to meet deliveries of munitions and raw materials to the Soviet Union is accepted by the Soviet Government with heartfelt gratitude as vital aid to the Soviet Union in its tremendous and onerous struggle against our common enemy—bloody Hitlerism.

On instructions from the Government of the U.S.S.R., I express complete agreement with your terms for granting the loan, repayment of which shall begin five years after the end of the war and continue over 10 years after expiration of the five-year period.

The Soviet Government is ready to do everything to supply the United States of America with such commodities and raw materials as are available and as the United States may need.

As regards your wish, Mr. President, that direct personal contact be established between you and me without delay if circumstances so require, I gladly join you in that wish and am ready, for my part, to do all in my power to bring it about.

Yours very sincerely,
J. STALIN

NOVEMBER 4, 1941

F. Roosevelt to J. V. Stalin

I am happy to inform you that medical supplies in the list prepared by the Medical Supplies Committee of the Three-Power Conference will be provided as rapidly as these supplies can be purchased and shipped, less such portion thereof as the British may provide. Conditions of American supply and production make impossible the immediate purchase of large amounts of certain items requested, but 25 percent of the total list can be provided within thirty to sixty days and the balance in installments during the next eight months.

The American Red Cross is prepared to provide approximately one-third of the total list at an approximate cost of $5,000,000 as a gift of the American people. Acting on my instructions, the American Red Cross will procure these supplies with funds placed at my disposal by the Congress and also funds contributed by the American people for relief in the Soviet Union. As the American Red Cross must account to the Congress and to its contributors for the use of these funds and supplies, Wardwell, the Chairman of their Delegation, outlined in a letter to Mr. Kolesnikov, of the Soviet Alliance, the kind of cooperative arrangement between the Red Cross societies of our respective countries which is desired. The Red Cross is also transmitting a message to Mr. Kolesnikov today pointing out the importance of reasonable observation by the American Red Cross representative of the distribution made of its supplies subject, of course, to all appropriate military considerations. I would deeply appreciate it if your Government can assure me that the desired arrangements are acceptable. I may point out that the procedures proposed by the American Red Cross are the same which are followed with regard to their assistance in Great Britain and other countries.

On the basis indicated, the American Red Cross is prepared to consider further substantial assistance in the Soviet Union as needs develop and requests are made.

NOVEMBER 6, 1941

Sent on November 14, 1941

Personal Message from J. Stalin to Mr. Roosevelt

Your message about the favorable decision taken by the American Red Cross concerning delivery of medical supplies reached me on November 11.

The Soviet Government has no objection to establishing

the organizational forms of cooperation between the Red Cross societies of our two countries, it being understood that it will be organized in accordance with the exchange of letters the text of which was agreed early in November by Red Cross representatives of both countries in Kuibyshev.

STALIN

Received on April 12, 1942

Personal Message from the President to Mr. Stalin

It is unfortunate that geographical distance makes it practically impossible for you and me to meet at this time. Such a meeting of minds in personal conversation would be useful to the conduct of the war against Hitlerism. Perhaps if things go as well as we hope, you and I could spend a few days together next summer near our common border off Alaska. But, in the meantime, I regard it as of the utmost military importance that we have the nearest possible approach to an exchange of views.

I have in mind a very important military proposal involving the utilization of our armed forces in a manner to relieve your critical Western Front. This objective carries great weight with me.

Therefore, I wish you would consider sending Mr. Molotov and a General upon whom you rely to Washington in the immediate future. Time is of the essence if we are to help in an important way. We will furnish them with a good transport plane so that they should be able to make the round trip in two weeks.

I do not want by such a trip to go over the head of my friend, Mr. Litvinov, in any way, as he will understand, but we can gain time by the visit I propose.

I suggest this procedure not only because of the secrecy, which is so essential, but because I need your advice before we determine with finality the strategic course of our common military action.

I have sent Hopkins to London relative to this proposal.

The American people are thrilled by the magnificent fighting of your armed forces, and we want to help you in the destruction of Hitler's armies and material more than we are doing now.

I send you my sincere regards.

ROOSEVELT

Received on December 16, 1941

F. Roosevelt to J. V. Stalin

(Retranslated)

It is extremely important, in my view, to take immediate steps for the purpose of paving the way not only for joint operations in the coming weeks, but also for the final defeat of Hitlerism. I should like very much to see you and talk it over personally with you, but since at the moment this is impossible, I am taking three preliminary steps which, I hope, will lead to more permanent joint planning.

I am suggesting to Generalissimo Chiang Kai-shek that he should immediately convene in Chungking a conference of Chinese, Soviet, British, Dutch, and U.S. representatives. This group should get together not later than December 17 and report the results to their Governments absolutely confidentially by Saturday, December 20. That should give us a preliminary idea of the general problem from the Chungking angle.

2. I am asking the British to call a naval conference at Singapore which would by Saturday, December 20, submit its report to be compiled chiefly in terms of operations in the southern zone.

3. I would be very glad if you talked this over personally with the United States, British, and Chinese Ambassadors in Moscow and let me know your proposals for the whole problem by Saturday, the 20th.

4. In a week or so I will be discussing the same problems with the British Missions here and will inform you of the situation as it appears from here. I had a good talk with Litvinov, and I fully understand your immediate tasks. I want to tell you once more about the genuine enthusiasm throughout the United States for the success of your armies in the defense of your great nation. I flatter myself with the hope that the preliminary conferences I have scheduled for the next week will lead to a more permanent organization for the planning of our efforts. Hopkins and I send you our personal warm regards.

ROOSEVELT

Sent on December 17, 1941

J. V. Stalin to F. Roosevelt

I received your message on December 16. It did not indicate the aims of the conferences to be called in Chungking and Moscow, and as they were to open overnight, I saw fit, when I met Mr. Eden, who had just arrived in Moscow, to ask him what those aims were and whether the two conferences could be put off for a while. It appeared, however, that Mr. Eden was not posted either. I should like, therefore, to have the appropriate elucidations from you in order to ensure the results expected from Soviet participation.

Thank you for the sentiments expressed over the Soviet armies' successes.

I wish you success in the struggle against the aggression in the Pacific.

Personal warm regards to you and Mr. Hopkins.

STALIN

PART II

1942

Received on February 13, 1942

F. Roosevelt to J. V. Stalin

I am much pleased that your Government has expressed its willingness to receive my old and trusted friend, Admiral Standley, as the Ambassador of the United States. He and I have been closely associated for many years, and I have complete confidence in him. I recommend him to you not only as a man of integrity and energy but also as one who is appreciative of and an admirer of the accomplishments of the Soviet Union, which, you will recall, he visited last year with Mr. Harriman. Admiral Standley has, since his return from Moscow, already done much to further understanding in the United States of the situation in the Soviet Union, and with his rich background and his knowledge of the problems which are facing our respective countries, I am sure that with your cooperation his efforts to bring them still more close together will meet with success.

My attention has just been called to the fact that the Soviet Government has placed requisitions with us for supplies and munitions of a value which will exceed the billion dollars which were placed at its disposal last autumn under the Lease-Lend Act following an exchange of letters between us. Therefore, I propose that under this same Act a second billion dollars be placed at the disposal of your Government upon the same conditions as those upon which the first billion were allocated. Should you have any counter-suggestions to offer with regard to the terms under which the second billion dollars should be made available, you may be sure that careful and sympathetic consideration will be given them. It may, in any event, prove mutually desirable later to review such financial arrangements as we may enter into now to meet changing conditions.

Sent on February 18, 1942

J. V. Stalin to F. Roosevelt

This is to acknowledge receipt of yours of February 13. I should like first of all to point out that I share your conviction that the efforts of the new U.S. Ambassador to Moscow, Admiral Standley, whom you hold in such high esteem, to bring our two countries still closer together, will be crowned with success.

Your decision, Mr. President, to grant the Government of the U.S.S.R. another $1,000,000,000 under the Lend-Lease Act on the same terms as the first $1,000,000,000, is accepted by the Soviet Government with sincere gratitude. With reference to the matter raised by you, I would like to say that, in order not to delay decision, the Soviet Government will not at the moment raise the matter of revising the terms for the second $1,000,000,000 to be granted to the Soviet Union, nor call for taking due account of the extreme strain placed on the U.S.S.R. by the war against our common foe. At the same time, I fully agree with you and hope that later we shall jointly fix the moment when it will be mutually desirable to revise the financial agreements now being concluded, in order to take special account of the circumstances pointed out above.

I take this opportunity to draw your attention to the fact

that in using the loan extended to the U.S.S.R. the appropriate Soviet agencies are encountering great difficulties as far as shipping the munitions and materials purchased in the U.S.A. is concerned. In these circumstances we think that the most useful system is the one effectively used in shipping munitions from Britain to Archangel, a system not introduced so far with regard to supplies from the U.S.A. In keeping with this system, the British military authorities supplying the munitions and materials select the ships, supervise their loading in harbor and convoying to the ports of destination. The Soviet Government would be most grateful if the same system of delivering munitions and convoying the ships to Soviet harbors were adopted by the U.S. Government.

Yours very sincerely,
J. STALIN

_____

Sent on April 20, 1942

J. V. Stalin to F. Roosevelt

Thank you for the message which I received in Moscow a few days ago.

The Soviet Government agrees that it is essential to arrange a meeting between V. M. Molotov and you for an exchange of views on the organization of a second front in Europe in the near future. Molotov can arrive in Washington not later than May 10-15, accompanied by an appropriate military representative.

It goes without saying that Molotov will also go to London to exchange views with the British Government.

I have no doubt that I shall be able to have a personal meeting with you, to which I attach great importance, especially in view of the big problems of organizing the defeat of Hitlerism that confront our two countries.

Please accept my sincere regards and wishes for success in the struggle against the enemies of the United States of America.

J. STALIN

For Mr. Stalin

We are having grave difficulties with the northern convoy route and have informed Litvinov of the complications. You may be sure, however, that no effort will be omitted to get as many ships off as possible.

I have heard of Admiral Standley's cordial reception by you and wish to express my appreciation.

I am looking forward to seeing Molotov, and the moment I hear of the route, we shall make preparations to provide immediate transportation. I do hope Molotov can stay with me in the White House while he is in Washington, but we can make a private home nearby available if that is desired.

ROOSEVELT

MAY 4, 1942

Sent on May 15, 1942

J. V. Stalin to F. Roosevelt

Thank you for the message delivered by M. M. Litvinov. In connection with the present difficulties in sailing and escorting ships to the U.S.S.R., I have already approached Prime Minister Churchill for his help in overcoming them as quickly as possible. As the delivery of cargoes from the U.S.A. and Britain in May is a pressing matter, I address the same request to you, Mr. President.

V. M. Molotov will leave for the U.S.A. and Britain a few days later than planned—on account of weather vagaries. It appears that he can fly in a Soviet aircraft—both to Britain and the U.S.A. I should add that the Soviet Government thinks it necessary for Molotov to travel without any press publicity until he returns to Moscow, as was done in the case of Mr. Eden's visit to Moscow last December.

As to Molotov's place of residence in Washington, both he and I thank you for your offer.

J. STALIN

F. Roosevelt to J. V. Stalin

The situation, which is developing in the Northern Area of the Pacific Ocean and in the Alaskan Area, presents tangible evidence that the Japanese Government may be taking steps to carry out operations against the Soviet Maritime Provinces. Should such an attack materialize, the United States is ready to assist the Soviet Union with American air power provided the Soviet Union makes available to it suitable landing fields in the Siberian Area. The efforts of the Soviet Union and of the United States would, of course, have to be carefully coordinated in order promptly to carry out such an operation.

Ambassador Litvinov has informed me that you have signified your approval of the movement of American planes via Alaska and Northern Siberia to the Western Front, and I am pleased to receive this news. I am of the opinion that in our common interests it is essential that detailed information be immediately initiated between our joint Army, Navy, and Air representatives in order to meet this new danger in the Pacific. I feel that the question is so urgent as to warrant granting to the representatives of the Soviet Union and of the United States full power to initiate action and to make definite plans. For this reason, I propose that you and I appoint such representatives and that we direct them immediately to confer in Moscow and Washington.

JUNE 17, 1942

Received on July 18, 1942

W. Churchill to J. V. Stalin

We began running small convoys to North Russia in August 1941, and until December the Germans did not take any steps to interfere with them. From February 1942, the size of the convoys was increased, and the Germans then moved a considerable force of U-boats and a large number of aircraft to Northern Norway and made determined attacks on the convoys. By giving the convoys the strongest possible escort of destroyers and anti-submarine craft, the convoys got through with varying but not prohibitive losses. It is evident that the Germans were dissatisfied with the results which were being achieved by means of aircraft and U-boats alone, because they began to use their surface forces against the convoys. Luckily for us, however, at the outset they made use of their heavy surface forces to the westward of Bear Island and their submarines to the eastward.

The Home Fleet was thus in a position to prevent an attack by enemy surface forces. Before the May convoy was sent off, the Admiralty warned us that losses would be very severe if, as was expected, the Germans employed their surface forces to the eastward of Bear Island. We decided to sail the convoy. An attack by surface ships did not materialize, and the convoy got through with a loss of one-sixth, chiefly from air attack. In the case of the last convoy, which is numbered P.Q. 17, however, the Germans at last used their forces in the manner we had always feared. They concentrated their U-boats to the westward of Bear Island and reserved their surface forces for attack to the eastward of Bear Island. The final story of P.Q. 17 convoy is not yet clear. At the moment, only four ships have arrived at Archangel, but six others are in Nova Zemlya harbors. The latter may however be attacked from the air separately. At the best, therefore, only one-third will have survived.

I must explain the dangers and difficulties of these convoy operations when the enemy battle squadron takes its station in the extreme North. We do not think it right to risk our Home Fleet eastward of Bear Island or where it can be brought under the attack of the airmen of German shore-based aircraft. If one or two of our very few most powerful types were to be lost or even seriously damaged while the *Tirpitz* and her consorts, soon to be joined by the *Scharnhorst*, remained in action, the whole command of the Atlantic would be lost. Besides affecting the food supplies by which we live, our war effort would be crippled; and, above all, the great convoys of American troops across the ocean, rising presently to as many as 80,000 in a month, would be prevented and the building up of a really strong second front in 1943 rendered impossible.

My naval advisers tell me that if they had the handling of the German surface, submarine, and air forces in present circumstances, they would guarantee the complete destruction of any convoy to North Russia. They have not been able so far to hold out hopes that convoys attempting to make the passage in perpetual daylight would fare better than P.Q. 17. It is therefore with the greatest regret that we have reached the conclusion that to attempt to run the next convoy, P.Q. 18, would bring no benefit to you and would only involve a dead loss to the common cause. At the same time, I give you my assurance that if we can devise arrangements which give a reasonable chance of at least a fair proportion of the contents of the convoys reaching you, we will start them again at once. The crux of the problem is to make the Barents Sea as dangerous for German warships as they make it for ourselves. This is what we should aim at doing with our joint resources. I should like to send a senior officer shortly to North Russia to confer with your officers and make a plan.

Meanwhile we are prepared to dispatch immediately to the Persian Gulf some of the ships which were to have sailed in P.Q. convoy. The selection of ships would be made with the Soviet authorities in London, in order that priorities of cargo may be agreed. If fighter aircraft (Hurricanes and Aircobras) are selected, can you operate and maintain them on the Southern Front? We could undertake to assemble them at Basra. We hope to increase the through-clearance capacity of the Trans-Iranian routes so as to reach 75,000 tons monthly by October, and are making efforts to obtain a further increase. We are asking the United States Government to help us by expediting the dispatch of rolling stock and trucks. An increased volume of traffic would be handled at once if you would agree to American trucks for the U.S.S.R., now being assembled in the Persian Gulf, being used as a shuttle service for transporting goods by road between the Gulf and the Caspian. In order to ensure the full use of capacity, we agree to raise the figure of loads due to arrive in September to 95,000 tons and October to 100,000 tons, both exclusive of trucks and aircraft.

Your telegram to me on June 20th referred to combined operations in the North. The obstacles to sending further convoys at the present time equally prevent our sending land forces and air forces for operations in Northern Norway. But our officers should forthwith consider together what combined operations may be possible in or after October, when there is a reasonable amount of darkness. It would be better if you could send your officers here, but if this is impossible, ours will come to you.

In addition to a combined operation in the North, we are studying how to help on your southern flank. If we can beat back Rommel, we might be able to send powerful air forces in the autumn to operate on the left of your line. The difficulties of maintaining these forces over the Trans-Iranian route without reducing your supplies will clearly be considerable, but I hope to put detailed proposals before you in the near future. We must first beat Rommel. The battle is now intense.

Let me once again express my thanks for the forty Bostons. The Germans are constantly sending more men and aircraft to Africa; but large reinforcements are approaching General Auchinleck, and the impending arrival of strong British and American heavy bomber aircraft forces should give security to the Eastern Mediterranean as well as obstruct Rommel's supply ports of Tobruk and Benghazi.

I am sure it would be in our common interest, Premier Stalin, to have the three divisions of Poles you so kindly offered join their compatriots in Palestine, where we can arm them fully. These would play a most important part in the future fighting, as well as in keeping the Turks in good heart by a sense of growing numbers to the southward. I hope this project of yours, which we greatly value, will not fall to the ground on account of the Poles wanting to bring with the troops a considerable mass of their women and children, who are largely dependent on the rations of the Polish soldiers. The feeding of these dependents will be a considerable burden to us. We think it well worthwhile bearing that burden for the sake of forming this Polish army which will be used faithfully for our common advantage. We are very hard up for food ourselves in the Levant area, but there is enough in India if we can bring it there.

If we do not get the Poles, we should have to fill their places by drawing on preparations now going forward on a vast scale for Anglo-American mass invasion of the Continent. These preparations have already led the Germans to withdraw two heavy bomber groups from South Russia to France. Believe me, there is nothing that is useful and sensible that we and the Americans will not do to help you in your grand struggle. The President and I are ceaselessly searching for means of overcoming the extraordinary difficulties which the geography, seawater, and the enemy's air power interpose. I have shown this telegram to the President.

Sent on July 13, 1942

F. Roosevelt to J. V. Stalin

In connection with my message to you of June 17, I wish to emphasize that if the delivery of aircraft from the United States to the Soviet Union could be effected through Alaska and Siberia instead of across Africa, as is now the practice, a great deal of time would be saved. Furthermore, the establishment of a ferry service through Siberia would permit the delivery by air of short-range aircraft to the Soviet Union instead of by sea, as is now the case.

If landing fields can be constructed in the Siberian area and meteorological and navigational facilities can be established to connect up with the appropriate American air services, I am prepared to instruct the American ferry crews to deliver aircraft to you at Lake Baikal. This air route could be easily connected up with the landing fields leading into the Vladivostok area. In the event of a Japanese attack on the Soviet Maritime Provinces, such a Siberian airway would permit the United States quickly to transfer American aircraft units to the latter area for the purpose of coming to the assistance of the Soviet Union.

From the studies I have made of the problems involved in the establishment of a Siberian-Lake Baikal air service, it is clear that certain rivers which flow into the Arctic Ocean would have to be utilized for the shipping into Eastern Siberia of such bulky goods as fuel, as well as machinery, needed for the construction of the landing fields. The reason why I am communicating with you before receiving an answer to my message of June 17 is dictated by the necessity for immediate action, since this freight must be moved while the rivers in question are free of ice—that is, during the next few weeks.

If you are in agreement with the urgency and importance of this air route, I request that in order to expedite its development you authorize an American airplane to make a survey and experimental flight from Alaska over the proposed route for the purpose of ascertaining what equipment and supplies would be needed to construct the necessary landing fields and to establish the essential navigational services. Civilian clothes would be worn by the personnel making this flight, and they would, in fact, conduct the flight as personnel of a commercial agency. Furthermore, all necessary measures would be taken to make sure that the personnel in no way would be identified with the military services of the United States. One or two Soviet officers or officials could, of course, be taken on the American plane at Nome, Alaska.

The flight would not be in lieu of the conversations of the joint Army, Navy, and Air representatives of the United States and the Soviet Union as recommended in my message of June 17. It would be conducted for the sole purpose of enabling these representatives to enter into their discussions with more accurate and detailed information of the problems involved than would otherwise be the case.

J U N E   2 3 ,   1 9 4 2

Sent on July 1, 1942

J. V. Stalin to F. Roosevelt

With reference to your latest messages, I should like to tell you that I fully concur with you as to the advisability of using the Alaska-Siberia route for U.S. aircraft deliveries to the Western Front. The Soviet Government has, therefore, issued instructions for completing at the earliest possible date the preparations now under way in Siberia to receive aircraft, that is, for adapting the existing airfields and providing them with additional facilities. As to whose pilots should fly the aircraft from Alaska. I think the task can be entrusted, as the State Department once suggested, to Soviet pilots who could travel to Nome or some other suitable place at the appointed time. An appropriate group of those pilots could be instructed to carry out the survey flight proposed by you. To fully ensure reception of the aircraft, we should like to know the number of planes which the U.S.A. is allocating for dispatch to the Western Front by that route.

As to your proposal for a meeting between U.S. and Soviet Army and Navy representatives to exchange information, if necessary, the Soviet Government is in agreement and would prefer to have the meeting in Moscow.

RECEIVED ON AUGUST 19, 1942

Sent on July 18, 1942

J. V. Stalin to F. Roosevelt

Your message on the designation of Major-General F. Bradley, Captain Duncan and Colonel Michela as the U.S. representatives at the Moscow conference has reached me. The U.S. delegates will be given every assistance in carrying out their assignment.

On the Soviet side, the conference will be attended by Major-General Sterligov, Colonel Kabanov, and Colonel Levandovich.

As regards the survey flight, we could in the next few days send a plane from Krasnoyarsk to Nome—I mean an American twin-engine aircraft—which could take on the U.S. officers on its way back from Nome.

I take this opportunity to thank you for the news about the dispatch of an additional hundred and fifteen tanks to the U.S.S.R.

I consider it my duty to warn you that, according to our experts at the front, U.S. tanks catch fire very easily when hit from behind or from the side by anti-tank rifle bullets. The reason is that the high-grade gasoline used forms inside the tank a thick layer of highly inflammable fumes. German tanks also use gasoline, but of low grade, which yields smaller quantities of fumes—hence, they are more fireproof. Our experts think that the diesel makes the best tank motor.

F. Roosevelt to J. V. Stalin

I have received your message regarding the proposed survey flight from Alaska and the Moscow conference. Members of the survey flight will be in Alaska and ready to depart by August first. In this connection, a four-engine bomber will be at Nome in the event that it is required.

I greatly appreciate your report on the difficulties experienced at the front with American tanks. It will be most helpful to our tank experts in eradicating the trouble with this model to have this information. The fire hazard in future models will be reduced, however, as they will operate on a lower-octane fuel.

J U L Y   2 3 ,   1 9 4 2

F. Roosevelt to J. V. Stalin

Knowledge has come to me which I feel is definitely authentic that the Government of Japan has decided not to undertake military operations against the Union of Soviet

Socialist Republics at this time. This, I believe, means postponement of any attack on Siberia until the spring of next year. Will you be kind enough to give this information to your visitor?

AUGUST 5, 1942

J. V. Stalin to W. Churchill
Memorandum

As a result of the exchange of views in Moscow on August 12, I have established that Mr. Churchill, the British Prime Minister, considers it impossible to open a second front in Europe in 1942.

It will be recalled that the decision to open a second front in Europe in 1942 was reached at the time of Molotov's visit to London, and found expression in the agreed Anglo-Soviet Communiqué released on June 12 last.

It will be recalled further that the opening of a second front in Europe was designed to divert German forces from the Eastern Front to the West, to set up in the West a major center of resistance to the German fascist forces and thereby ease the position of the Soviet troops on the Soviet-German front in 1942.

Needless to say, the Soviet High Command, in planning its summer and autumn operations, counted on a second front being opened in Europe in 1942.

It will be readily understood that the British Government's refusal to open a second front in Europe in 1942 delivers a moral blow to Soviet public opinion, which had hoped that the second front would be opened, complicates the position of the

Red Army at the front and injures the plans of the Soviet High Command.

I say nothing of the fact that the difficulties in which the Red Army is involved through the refusal to open a second front in 1942 are bound to impair the military position of Britain and the other Allies.

I and my colleagues believe that the year 1942 offers the most favorable conditions for a second front in Europe, seeing that nearly all the German forces—and their crack troops, too—are tied down on the Eastern Front, while only negligible forces, and the poorest, too, are left in Europe. It is hard to say whether 1943 will offer as favorable conditions for opening a second front as 1942. For this reason we think that it is possible and necessary to open a second front in Europe in 1942. Unfortunately, I did not succeed in convincing the British Prime Minister of this, while Mr. Harriman, the U.S. President's representative at the Moscow talks, fully supported the Prime Minister.

J. STALIN

A U G U S T 1 3 , 1 9 4 2

F. Roosevelt to J. V. Stalin

I regret indeed that I was unable to have been with you and Mr. Churchill in the conferences which have recently taken place in Moscow. The urgent needs of the military situation, especially insofar as the Soviet-German front is concerned, are well known to me.

I am of the opinion that it will be difficult for the Japanese to dislodge us from the vantage point which we have gained in the area of the Southwest Pacific. Although the naval losses of our forces were considerable in that area, the advantages which we have gained will justify them, and I can assure you we are going to press them in a vigorous manner. I well realize, on the other hand, that the real enemy of both our countries is Germany, and that, at the earliest possible moment, it will be necessary for both our countries to bring our power and forces to bear against Hitler. Just as soon as it is humanly possible to assemble the transportation you may be sure that this will be done.

In the interim, there will leave the United States for the Soviet Union during the month of August, over 1,000 tanks, and, at the same time, other strategic materials are going forward, including aircraft.

The fact that the Soviet Union is bearing the brunt of the fighting and losses during the year 1942 is well understood by the United States, and I may state that we greatly admire the magnificent resistance which your country has exhibited. We are coming as quickly and as strongly to your assistance as we possibly can, and I hope that you will believe me when I tell you this.

———

Sent on August 22, 1942

J. V. Stalin to F. Roosevelt

Your message of August 19 received. I, too, regret that you were unable to take part in the talks which Mr. Churchill and I recently had.

With reference to what you say about the dispatch of tanks and other strategic materials from the United States in August, I should like to emphasize our special interest in receiving

U.S. aircraft and other weapons, as well as trucks in the greatest numbers possible. It is my hope that every step will be taken to ensure early delivery of the cargoes to the Soviet Union, particularly over the northern sea route.

His Excellency Joseph Stalin, President of the Soviet of People's Commissars of the USSR

Moscow

My dear Mr. Stalin,

I am giving this letter of presentation to you to General Patrick J. Hurley, former Secretary of War and at present United States Minister to New Zealand.

General Hurley is returning to his post in New Zealand, and I have felt it to be of the highest importance that, prior to his return, he should be afforded the opportunity of visiting Moscow and of learning, so far as may be possible, through his own eyes, the most significant aspects of our present world strategy. I wish him in this way, as a result of his personal experiences, to be able to assure the Government of New Zealand and likewise the Government of Australia that the most effective manner in which the United Nations can join in defeating Hitler is through the rendering of all possible assistance to the gallant Russian armies, who have so brilliantly withstood the attacks of Hitler's armies.

I have requested General Hurley likewise to visit Egypt, as well as Iran and Iraq, in order that he might thus personally familiarize himself with that portion of the Middle East and see for himself the campaign which is being carried on in that area.

As you know, the Governments of Australia and of New Zealand have been inclined to believe that it was imperative that an immediate and all-out attack should be made by the United Nations against Japan. What I wish General Hurley to be able to say to those two Governments after his visit to the Soviet Union is that the best strategy for the United Nations to pursue is for them first to join in making possible the defeat of Hitler, and that this is the best and surest way of ensuring the defeat of Japan.

I send you my heartiest congratulations on the magnificent achievements of the Soviet armies and my best wishes for your continued welfare.

Believe me

Yours very sincerely,
Franklin D. ROOSEVELT

OCTOBER 5, 1942

From Premier Stalin to the President, Mr. Roosevelt

In taking this opportunity to send you a personal message through the courtesy of Mr. Standley, who is leaving for Washington, I should like to say a few words about U.S. military deliveries to the U.S.S.R.

The difficulties of delivery are reported to be due primarily to shortage of shipping. To remedy the shipping situation, the Soviet Government would be prepared to agree to a certain curtailment of U.S. arms deliveries to the Soviet Union. We should be prepared temporarily fully to renounce deliveries of tanks, guns, ammunition, pistols, etc. At the same time, however, we are badly in need of increased deliveries of modern fighter aircraft—such as Aircobras—and certain other supplies. It should be borne in mind that the Kittyhawk is no match for the modern German fighter.

It would be very good if the U.S.A. could ensure the monthly delivery of at least the following items: 500 fighters, 8,000 to 10,000 trucks, 5,000 tons of aluminum, and 4,000 to 5,000 tons of explosives. Besides, we need, within 12 months, two million tons of grain (wheat) and as much as we can have of fats, concentrated foods, and canned meat. We could bring in a considerable part of the food supplies in Soviet ships via Vladivostok if the U.S.A. consented to turn over to the U.S.S.R. 20 to 30 ships, at the least, to replenish our fleet. I have talked this over with Mr. Willkie, feeling certain that he will convey it to you.

As regards the situation at the front, you are undoubtedly aware that in recent months our position in the South, particularly in the Stalingrad area, has deteriorated due to shortage of aircraft, mostly fighters. The Germans have bigger stocks of aircraft than we anticipated. In the South they have at least a twofold superiority in the air, which makes it impossible for us to protect our troops. War experience has shown that the bravest troops are helpless unless protected against air attack.

OCTOBER 7, 1942

Received on November 5, 1942

Personal and Secret Message from the Prime Minister, Mr. Winston Churchill, to M. Stalin

I promised to tell you when our army in Egypt had gained a decisive victory over Rommel. General Alexander now reports that enemy's front is broken and that he is retreating westwards in considerable disorder. Apart from the troops in the main battle, there are six Italian and two German divisions in the desert to the south of our advance along the coast. These have very little mechanical transport or supplies, and it is possible that a very heavy toll will be taken in the next few days. Besides this, Rommel's only line of retreat is along the coastal road which is now crammed with troops and transport and under continuous attack of our greatly superior Air Force.

2. *Most Secret*. For yourself alone. "Torch" is imminent on a very great scale. I believe political difficulties about which you expressed concern have been satisfactorily solved. The military movement is proceeding with precision.

3. I am most anxious to proceed with the placing of twenty British and American Squadrons on your southern flank as early as possible. President Roosevelt is in full accord, and there is no danger now of a disaster in Egypt. Before anything can be done, however, it is necessary that detailed arrangements should be made about landing grounds, etc., between your officers and ourselves. Kindly let me know as soon as possible how you would like this consultation to be arranged. The Squadrons it is proposed to send were stated in my telegram of October 9th, in accordance with which we have been making such preparations as were possible pending arrangements with you.

4. Let me further express to you, Premier Stalin, and to M. Molotov, our congratulations on the ever-glorious defense

of Stalingrad and on the decisive defeat of Hitler's second campaign against Russia. I should be glad to know from you how you stand in the Caucasus.

5. All good wishes for your anniversary.

Sent on November 8, 1942

Personal and Secret Message from Premier Stalin to Prime Minister Churchill

Your message reached me on November 5.

I congratulate you on the progress of the operation in Egypt and feel confident that now it will be possible to finish off the bands of Rommel and his Italian allies.

All of us here hope that "Torch" will be successful.

I am grateful to you for informing me that you and President Roosevelt have decided to send 20 British and American Squadrons to the Southern Front in the near future. Speedy dispatch of the 20 Squadrons will be a very valuable help. As to the conferences required in this connection and to the working out of specific measures by representatives of the British, American, and our own Air Forces, it would be best to hold the appropriate meetings first in Moscow, and then, if necessary, directly in the Caucasus. I have already been informed that the U.S. side is sending General Elmer E. Adler for the purpose. I shall expect to hear from you the name of the British appointee.

The situation on our Caucasian front has deteriorated somewhat compared with October. The Germans have succeeded in capturing Nalchik and are closing in on Vladikavkaz, where heavy fighting is now in progress. Our weak point there is shortage of fighter aircraft.

Thank you for your good wishes for the anniversary of the U.S.S.R.

Most Secret and Personal Message from the Prime Minister, Mr. Winston Churchill, to Premier Stalin

It gave me the very greatest pleasure to receive your warm and heartfelt congratulations. I regard our truthful personal relations as most important to the discharge of our duties to the great masses whose lives are at stake.

2. Although the President is unable with great regret to lend me the twelve American destroyers for which I asked, I have now succeeded in making arrangements to sail a convoy of over thirty ships from Iceland on December 22nd. The Admiralty will concert operations with your officers as before. The Germans have moved the bulk of their aircraft from North Norway to South Europe as a result of "Torch." On the other hand, German surface forces in Norway are still on guard. The Admiralty are pleased so far with the progress of the Q.P. convoy, which has been helped by bad weather and is now under the protection of our cruisers which have been sent out to meet it.

3. I have communicated to President Roosevelt some preliminary ideas about Turkey and have found that he independently had formed very similar views. It seems to me that we ought all of us to make a new intense effort to make Turkey enter the war on our side in the spring. For the purpose, I should like the United States to join in an Anglo-Soviet guar-

antee of the territorial integrity and status of Turkey. This would bring our three forces all into line; and the Americans count for a lot with the Turks. Secondly, we are already sending Turkey a considerable consignment of munitions, including 200 tanks from the Middle East. During the winter, by land route or coasting up the Levant, I shall keep on sending supplies of munitions to Turkey together, if permitted, with experts in plainclothes for training and maintenance purposes. Thirdly, I hope by early spring to assemble a considerable army in Syria drawn from our Eighth, Ninth and Tenth Armies, so as to go to help Turkey if either she were threatened or were willing to join us. It is evident that your operations in the Caucasus or north of it may also exercise a great influence. If we could get Turkey into the war, we could not only proceed with operations designed to open a shipping route to your left flank on the Black Sea, but we could also bomb heavily from Turkish bases the Rumanian oil fields which are of such vital importance to the Axis in view of your successful defense of main oil supplies in the Caucasus. The advantage of a move into Turkey is that it proceeds mainly by land and can be additional to offensive action in the Central Mediterranean, which will absorb our sea power and much of our air power.

4. I have agreed to President Roosevelt's suggestion that we each send in the near future, if agreeable to you, two high British officers and two Americans to Moscow to plan this part of the war in 1943. Pray let me know if you agree.

5. I hope you realize, Premier Stalin, that shipping is our limiting factor. In order to do "Torch" we have had to cut our Trans-Atlantic escorts so fine that the first half of November has been our worst month so far. We and the Americans have budgeted to lose at the rate of 700,000 tons a month and still improve our margin. Over the year the average loss has not been quite so bad as that, but this first fortnight in November is worse. You who have so much land may find it hard to realize that we can only live and fight in proportion to our sea communications.

6. Do not be disturbed about the rogue Darlan. We have thrown a large Anglo-American army into French North Africa and are getting a very firm grip. Owing to the non-resistance of the French Army and now to its increasing sup-

port we are perhaps fifteen days ahead of schedule. It is of the utmost consequence to get the Tunis tip and the naval base of Bizerta at the earliest moment. The leading elements of our First Army will probably begin their attack immediately. Once established there with overpowering air strength, we can bring the war home to Mussolini and his Fascist gang with an intensity not yet possible.

7. At the same time, by building up a strong Anglo-American army and air force in Great Britain and making continuous preparations along our southeastern and southern coasts, we keep the Germans pinned in the Pas de Calais, etc., and are ready to take advantage of any favorable opportunity. And all the time our bombers will be blasting Germany with ever-increasing violence. Thus the halter will tighten upon the guilty doomed.

8. The glorious news of your offensive is streaming in. We are watching it with breathless attention. Every good wish.

NOVEMBER 24, 1942

To President Roosevelt from Premier Stalin

My dear Mr. President,

Thank you very much for your letter, which reached me through General Hurley today. I have had a long talk with him on strategic matters. I think that he understood me and is now convinced of the soundness of the Allies' present strategy. He asked for an opportunity to visit one of our fronts, in particular the Caucasus. This opportunity will be provided.

No serious changes have occurred on the Soviet-German front in the past week. We plan to launch our winter campaign in the near future and are preparing for it. I shall keep you informed about it.

All of us here rejoice at the brilliant success of U.S. and British arms in North Africa. Congratulations on the victory. With all my heart I wish you further success.

Yours very sincerely,
STALIN

NOVEMBER 14, 1942

F. Roosevelt to J. V. Stalin

I am glad you have been so kind to General Hurley. As you can well recognize, I have had a problem in persuading the people of Australia and New Zealand that the menace of Japan can be most effectively met by destroying the Nazis first. General Hurley will be able to tell them at first hand how you and Churchill and I are in complete agreement on this.

Our recent battles in the Southwest Pacific make the position there more secure even though we have not yet eliminated attempts by the Japanese to extend their southward drive.

The American and British staffs are now studying further moves in the event that we secure the whole south shore of the Mediterranean from Gibraltar to Syria. Before any further step is taken, both Churchill and I want to consult with you and your staff, because whatever we do next in the Mediterranean

will have a definite bearing on your magnificent campaign and
your proposed moves this coming winter.

I do not have to tell you to keep up the good work. You are
doing that, and I honestly feel that things everywhere look
brighter.

> *With my warm regards,*
> *ROOSEVELT*

NOVEMBER 19, 1942

Sent on November 20, 1942

Personal and Secret Message
from Premier Stalin
to the President, Mr. Roosevelt

We have begun the offensive operations in the Stalingrad
area—in its southern and northwestern sectors. The objective
of the first stage is to seize the Stalingrad-Likhaya railway
and disrupt the communications of the Stalingrad group of
the German troops. In the northwestern sector the German
front has been pierced along a 22-kilometer line and along
a 12-kilometer line in the southern sector. The operation is
proceeding satisfactorily.

F. Roosevelt to J. V. Stalin

I want you to know that we have hit the Japs very hard in the Solomons. There is a probability that we have broken the backbone of the strength of their fleet, although they still have too many aircraft carriers to suit me, but we may well get some more of them soon.

We are in the Southwest Pacific with very heavy forces by air, land, and sea and we do not intend to play a waiting game. We are going to press our advantages.

I am sure we are sinking far more Jap ships and destroying more airplanes than they can build.

I am hopeful that we are going to drive the Germans out of Africa soon, and then we will give the Italians a taste of some real bombing, and I am quite sure they will never stand up under that kind of pressure.

The news from the Stalingrad area is most encouraging, and I send you my warmest congratulations.

NOVEMBER 26, 1942

Personal and Secret Message from Premier Stalin to President Roosevelt

Thank you for your message which reached me on November 27. I am glad to hear of your successes in the Solomons area and of the strong build-up of your forces in the Southwest Pacific.

Feeling certain of the speedy expulsion of Germans from North Africa, I trust that this will help in launching Allied offensive operations in Europe. The intensive air raids planned for Italy will no doubt be very useful.

We have achieved some success in the Stalingrad operation, largely facilitated by snowfall and fog which prevented the Germans from making full use of their aircraft.

We have decided to launch operations on the Central Front, too, to keep the enemy from moving his forces south.

I send you warm regards and best wishes to the U.S. Armed Forces.

NOVEMBER 28, 1942

Sent on November 27, 1942

Personal and Secret Message
from Premier Stalin
to President Roosevelt

Thank you for your message, received on November 21. I fully appreciate your desire to explain the military set-up to people in Australia and New Zealand, and your preoccupation with operations in the Southwest Pacific. As to the Mediterranean operations, which are making such favorable progress and are important in terms of changing the whole military situation in Europe, I share your view that the time is ripe for appropriate consultations between the General Staffs of the U.S.A., Great Britain, and the U.S.S.R.

Heartfelt regards and best wishes for further success in your offensive.

Sent on November 27, 1942

Personal and Secret Message from Premier Stalin to the Prime Minister, Mr. Churchill

Thank you for your message, which I received on November 25. I fully share your view that it is highly important to promote our personal relations.

I express gratitude for the steps you are taking to send another large convoy to Archangel. I realize that at the moment this is particularly difficult for you, especially in view of the considerable operations by the British fleet in the Mediterranean.

I agree with you and President Roosevelt concerning the desirability of doing everything to bring Turkey into the war on our side in the spring. That, without a doubt, would mean a great deal for the speedy defeat of Hitler and his accomplices.

As for Darlan, I think the Americans have made skillful use of him to facilitate the occupation of North and West Africa. Military diplomacy should know how to use for the war aims not only the Darlans, but even the devil and his grandmother.

I have carefully read your communication saying that you and the Americans are continuing the preparations along your southeastern and southern coasts in order to keep the Germans pinned in the Pas de Calais, etc., and that you are ready to take advantage of any favorable opportunity. That, I hope, does not imply renunciation of your Moscow promise to open a second front in Western Europe in the spring of 1943.

I accept President Roosevelt's and your suggestion that we call a conference of representatives of our three Staffs in Moscow to make appropriate war plans for 1943. We are prepared to meet your representatives, and the Americans, whenever you like.

So far the Stalingrad operation is proceeding successfully, helped among other things by snowfall and fog which prevent full-scale action by German aircraft.

We are planning active operations on the Central Front one of these days in order to tie up the enemy and prevent him from moving forces south.

Fighting is developing both at Stalingrad and on the Central Front. At Stalingrad we have encircled a large group of German troops and hope to complete their destruction.

As is known, the Anglo-Soviet Treaty of May 26, 1942, provides that our two countries shall not negotiate a separate peace either with Germany or with her allies other than by mutual agreement. This, for me, is an inviolable provision.

I therefore consider it my duty, first, to inform you of the American proposal and, secondly, to ask your opinion on the matter.

I have no reason to believe that Finland really wants peace, that she has already resolved to break with Germany and is willing to offer acceptable terms. She has probably not yet broken loose from Hitler's clutches, if she wants at all to do so. The present rulers of Finland, who signed a peace treaty with the Soviet Union and then tore it up and, in alliance with Germany, attacked the Soviet Union, are hardly capable of breaking with Hitler.

Nevertheless, in view of the U.S. proposal, I considered it my duty to advise you of the foregoing.

F. Roosevelt to J. V. Stalin

The more I consider our mutual military situation and the necessity for reaching early strategic decisions, the more persuaded I am that you, Churchill and I should have an early meeting.

It seems to me that a conference of our military leaders alone will not be sufficient, first, because they could come to no ultimate decisions without our approval and, secondly, because I think we should come to some tentative understanding about the procedures which should be adopted in event of a German collapse.

My most compelling reason is that I am very anxious to have a talk with you. My suggestion would be that we meet secretly in some secure place in Africa that is convenient to all three of us. The time, about January 15th to 20th.

We would each of us bring a very small staff of our top army, air, and naval commanders.

I hope that you will consider this proposal favorably because I can see no other way of reaching the vital strategic decisions which should be made soon by all of us together. If the right decision is reached, we may, and I believe will, knock Germany out of the war much sooner than we anticipated.

I can readily fly, but I consider Iceland or Alaska out of the question at this time of the year. Some place can, I think, be found in Southern Algeria or at or near Khartoum where all visitors and press can be kept out. As a mere suggestion as to date, would you think of sometime around January 15.

DECEMBER 2, 1942

Sent on December 6, 1942

Personal and Secret Message
from Premier Stalin
to President Roosevelt

Your message reached me on December 5.

I welcome the idea of a meeting between the three heads of the Governments to establish a common strategy. To my great regret, however, I shall be unable to leave the Soviet Union. This is so crucial a moment that I cannot absent myself even for a single day. Just now major military operations—part of our winter campaign—are under way, nor will they be relaxed in January. It is more than likely that it will be the other way round.

Fighting is developing both at Stalingrad and on the Central Front. At Stalingrad we have encircled a large group of German troops and hope to complete their destruction.

Most Secret and Personal Message from the Prime Minister, Mr. Winston Churchill, to Premier Stalin

In your message to me of November 27th in the last sentence of paragraph 5 and also in your message of December 6th, you ask specifically about a second front in 1943. I am not able to reply to this question except jointly with the President of the United States. It was for this reason that I so earnestly desired a meeting between the three of us. We both understand the paramount military reasons which prevent you from leaving Russia while conducting your great operations. I am in constant communication with the President in order to see what can be done.

DECEMBER 12, 1942

F. Roosevelt to J. V. Stalin

I am deeply disappointed you feel you cannot get away for a conference in January. There are many matters of vital importance to be discussed between us. These relate not only to vital strategic decision, but also to things we should talk over in a tentative way in regard to emergency policies which we should be ready with, if, and when, conditions in Germany permit.

These would also include other matters relating to future policies about North Africa and the Far East which cannot be discussed by our military people alone.

I fully realize your strenuous situation now and in the immediate future and the necessity of your presence close to the fighting front. Therefore I want to suggest that we set a tentative date for meeting in North Africa about March 1.

DECEMBER 8, 1942

Sent on December 14, 1942

J. V. Stalin to F. Roosevelt

I, too, express deep regret at not being able to leave the Soviet Union in the immediate future, or even in early March. Front affairs simply will not let me do so. Indeed, they necessitate my continuous presence.

I do not know as yet what were the specific matters that you, Mr. President, and Mr. Churchill wanted discussed at our joint conference. Could we not discuss them by correspondence until we have an opportunity to meet? I think we shall not differ.

I feel confident that no time is being wasted, that the promise to open a second front in Europe, which you, Mr. President, and Mr. Churchill gave for 1942 or the spring of 1943 at the latest, will be kept and that a second front in Europe will really be opened jointly by Great Britain and the U.S.A. next spring.

With reference to the rumors about the Soviet attitude to the use of Darlan and people like him, I should like to tell you that as I and my colleagues see it, Eisenhower's policy towards Darlan, Boisson, Giraud and the others is absolutely sound. I consider it an important achievement that you have succeeded in winning Darlan and others to the Allied side against Hitler. Earlier I wrote the same to Mr. Churchill.

F. Roosevelt to J. V. Stalin

I am not clear as to just what has happened in regard to our offer of American air assistance in the Caucasus. I am fully willing to send units with American pilots and crews. I think they should operate by units under their American commanders, but each group would, of course, be under overall Russian command as to tactical objectives.

Please let me know your desires as soon as possible, as I truly want to help all I can.

Pursuit plane program would not be affected. What I refer to is essentially the bombing plane type which can be flown to the Caucasus.

DECEMBER 16, 1942

Sent on December 18, 1942

Personal and Secret Message from Premier Stalin to the U.S. President, Mr. Roosevelt

Thank you very much for the willingness to help us. The Anglo-American squadrons with crews are no longer needed in Transcaucasia. The main battles are being fought, and will be fought, on the Central Front and in the Voronezh area. I should be most grateful if you would expedite the despatch of aircraft, especially fighters, but without crews, whom you now need badly for use in the areas mentioned.

A feature of the Soviet Air Force is that we have more than enough pilots, but suffer from a shortage of machines.

F. Roosevelt to J. V. Stalin

In the event that Japan should attack Russia in the Far East, I am prepared to assist you in that theater with an American air force of approximately one hundred four-engine bombardment airplanes as early as practicable, provided that certain items of supply and equipment are furnished by Soviet authorities and that suitable operation facilities are prepared in advance.

Supply of our units must be entirely by air transport; hence it will be necessary for the Soviet Government to furnish such items as bombs, fuel, lubricants, transportation, shelter, heat, and other minor items to be determined.

Although we have no positive information that Japan will attack Russia, it does appear to be an eventual probability. Therefore, in order that we may be prepared for this contingency, I propose that the survey of air force facilities in the Far East, authorized by you to General Bradley on October 6 be made now, and that the discussions initiated on November 11 on your authority between General Bradley and General Korolenko be continued.

It is my intention to appoint General Bradley, who has my full confidence, to continue these discussions for the United States if you so agree. He will be empowered to explore for the United States every phase of combined Russo-American operations in the Far East theater and based upon his survey to recommend the composition and strength of our air forces, which will be allocated to assist you should the necessity arise.

He will also determine the extent of advance preparations practicable and necessary to ensure effective participation of our units promptly on initiation of hostilities. His party will not exceed twenty persons to fly into Russia in two American Douglas DC-3 type airplanes.

If this meets with your approval, I would suggest that they proceed from Alaska along the ferry route into Siberia, thence, under Russian direction, to the headquarters of the Soviet armies in the Far East, and thence to such other places in Russia as may be necessary to make their quiet survey and discuss operating plans.

It would be very helpful if an English-speaking Russian officer such as Captain Vladimir Ovnovin, Washington, or Captain Smolyarov in Moscow be detailed to accompany General Bradley as adjutant and liaison officer.

I seize this opportunity of expressing my admiration for the courage, stamina and military prowess of your great Russian armies as reported to me by General Bradley and as demonstrated by your great victories of the past month.

DECEMBER 30, 1942

F. Roosevelt to J. V. Stalin

Struggling side by side against powerful foes, thousands upon thousands of soldiers of those nations, large and small, which are united in defense of freedom and justice and human rights face the holiday season far from home, across oceans or continents, in fields of desert sand or winter snow, in jungles, forests, on warships or merchant vessels, on island ramparts from Iceland to the Solomons, in the Old and New worlds.

They strive to the limit of their strength, without regard for the clock or the calendar, to hold the enemy in check and to push him back. They strike mighty blows and receive blows in return. They fight the good fight in order that they may win victory which will bring to the world peace, freedom, and the advancement of human welfare.

With a deep and abiding sense of gratitude the Congress of the United States has, by a joint resolution, asked me to transmit on behalf of the people of the United States to the armed forces and auxiliary services of our Allies on land, on sea, and in the air, the best wishes and greetings of the season to them and to their families and a fervent hope and prayer for a speedy and complete victory and a lasting peace.

Accordingly, I shall be grateful to you if you will convey to your armed forces and auxiliary services, in the name of the Congress of the United States, in my own name, and in the name of the people of the United States, the cordial wishes and greetings and the hope and prayer expressed in the joint resolution.

PART III

1943

F. Roosevelt to J. V. Stalin

After reading your reply to my radio [message, ed.] concerning the Far East, I am afraid I did not make myself clear. As I previously explained reference South Caucasus, it is not practicable to send heavy bombers to Russia at this time other than in existing organized units. Our proposal regarding the one hundred planes referred to a situation which would occur if hostilities were actually to break out between Japan and Russia.

Under such conditions, we calculated that by regrouping our air units in the Pacific theater, one hundred planes in organized units could be concentrated in Eastern Siberia because their action as well as your battle there would enable us to reduce our air strength elsewhere in the Pacific theater.

My radio [message, ed.] was intended to be in the nature of anticipatory protective planning against a possibility only.

The immediate action recommended was in reference to the survey and discussions by General Bradley with Soviet officials.

Only by such preliminary survey and advance planning will it be possible to render reasonably prompt assistance in the event of an outbreak of hostilities in Siberia. I should like to send General Marshall to Moscow for a visit in the very near future, and if this can be arranged, I hope that you will be able to discuss this matter with him at that time.

He will be able to tell you about the current situation in Africa and also about planned operations for balance of this year in all war theaters. I think this will be very helpful, and he will have the latest news.

Meanwhile I would appreciate an early reply to my proposal of December 30 that General Bradley and his party proceed without delay to the Far East for survey and staff discussions.

My deep appreciation for the continuing advances of your armies. The principle of attrition of the enemy forces on all fronts is beginning to work.

JANUARY 8, 1943

F. Roosevelt to J. V. Stalin

I have arranged that two hundred C-47 transport planes be assigned to you in 1943 beginning in January.

Your mission here is being advised of the dates of delivery by months.

I am going to do everything I can to give you another one hundred, but you can definitely count on the two hundred planes referred to above.

JANUARY 9, 1943

Sent on January 5, 1943

Personal and Secret Message
from Premier Stalin
to President Roosevelt

Your message concerning the Far East received. I thank you for the readiness to send 100 bombers to the Far East for the Soviet Union. I must say, however, that what we need at present is aircraft, not in the Far East, where the U.S.S.R. is not fighting, but on a front where a most cruel war is being waged against the Germans, that is, on the Soviet-German front. The arrival of those aircraft without pilots—because we have a sufficient number of pilots—on the Southwestern or Central Front would play a notable part in the most important sectors of our struggle against Hitler.

As regards the course of the war on our fronts, so far our offensive is, on the whole, making satisfactory progress.

Received on January 27, 1943

From President Roosevelt and Prime Minister Churchill to Premier Stalin

We have been in conference with our military advisers and have decided on the operations which are to be undertaken by the American and British forces in the first nine months of 1943. We wish to inform you of our intentions at once. We believe that these operations, together with your powerful offensive, may well bring Germany to her knees in 1943. Every effort must be made to accomplish this purpose.

2. We are in no doubt that our correct strategy is to concentrate on the defeat of Germany with a view to achieving an early and decisive victory in the European theater. At the same time, we must maintain sufficient pressure on Japan to retain the initiative in the Pacific and the Far East and sustain China and prevent the Japanese from extending their aggression to other theaters such as your Maritime Provinces.

3. Our main desire has been to divert strong German land and air forces from the Russian front and to send Russia the maximum flow of supplies. We shall spare no exertion to send you material assistance in any case by every available route.

4. Our immediate intention is to clear the Axis out of North Africa and set up naval and air installations to open:

(1) an effective passage through the Mediterranean for military traffic, and

(2) an intensive bombardment of important Axis targets in Southern Europe.

5. We have made the decision to launch large-scale amphibious operations in the Mediterranean at the earliest possible moment. The preparation for these operations is now under way and will involve a considerable concentration of forces, including landing craft and shipping, in Egypt and the North Africa ports. In addition, we shall concentrate within the United Kingdom a strong American land and air force. These, combined with the British forces in the United Kingdom, will prepare themselves to re-enter the continent of Europe as soon as practicable. These concentrations will certainly be known to our enemies, but they will not know where or when or on what scale we propose striking. They will, therefore, be compelled to divert both land and air forces to all the shores of France, the Low Countries, Corsica, Sardinia, Sicily and the Levant, and Italy, Yugoslavia, Greece, Crete, and the Dodecanese.

6. In Europe we shall increase the Allied bomber offensive from the United Kingdom against Germany at a rapid rate, and by midsummer it should be double its present strength. Our experiences to date have shown that day bombing attacks result in the destruction of, and damage to, large numbers of German fighter aircraft. We believe that an increased tempo and weight of daylight and night attacks will lead to greatly increased material and moral damage in Germany and rapidly deplete German fighter strength. As you are aware, we are already containing more than half the German Air Force in Western Europe and the Mediterranean. We have no doubt that our intensified and diversified bombing offensive, together with the other operations which we are undertaking, will compel further withdrawals of German air and other forces from the Russian front.

7. In the Pacific it is our intention to eject the Japanese from Rabaul within the next few months and thereafter to exploit the success in the general direction of Japan. We also intend to increase the scale of our operations in Burma in order to reopen this channel of supply to China. We intend to increase our Air Forces in China at once. We shall not, however, allow our offensives against Japan to jeopardize our capacity to take advantage of every opportunity that may present itself for the decisive defeat of Germany in 1943.

8. Our ruling purpose is to bring to bear upon Germany

and Italy the maximum forces by land, sea and air which can be physically applied.

Sent on January 13, 1943

Personal and Secret Message from Premier Stalin to President Roosevelt

Thank you for the decision to send 200 transport planes to the Soviet Union.

As to sending bomber units to the Far East, I have already pointed out in my previous messages that what we need is not air force units, but planes without pilots, because we have more than enough pilots of our own. Secondly, we need your help in the way of aircraft not in the Far East, where the U.S.S.R. is not in a state of war, but on the Soviet-German front, where the need for aircraft aid is particularly great.

I was rather surprised at your proposal that General Bradley should inspect Russian military objectives in the Far East and elsewhere in the U.S.S.R. It should be perfectly obvious that only Russians can inspect Russian military objectives, just as U.S. military objectives can be inspected by none but Americans. There should be no unclarity in this matter.

Concerning General Marshall's visit to the U.S.S.R., I must say I am not quite clear about his mission. Kindly advise me of the purpose of the visit so that I can consider the matter with full understanding and reply accordingly.

My colleagues are upset by the fact that the operations in North Africa have come to a standstill and, I gather, for a long time, too. Would you care to comment on the matter?

Sent on January 30, 1943

Personal and Secret Message from Premier Stalin to the President, Mr. Roosevelt, and the Prime Minister, Mr. Churchill

Your friendly joint message reached me on January 27. Thank you for informing me of the Casablanca decisions about the operations to be undertaken by the U.S. and British armed forces in the first nine months of 1943. Assuming that your decisions on Germany are designed to defeat her by opening a second front in Europe in 1943, I should be grateful if you would inform me of the concrete operations planned and of their timing.

As to the Soviet Union, I can assure you that the Soviet armed forces will do all in their power to continue the offensive against Germany and her allies on the Soviet-German front. We expect to finish our winter campaign, circumstances permitting, in the first half of February. Our troops are tired, they are in need of rest, and they will hardly be able to carry on the offensive beyond that period.

Most Secret and Personal Message from Premier Stalin to the President, Mr. Roosevelt

On February 12 I received from Mr. Churchill a message giving additional information on the decisions taken by the two of you at Casablanca. Since, according to Mr. Churchill, his message is a common reply giving your opinion as well, I should like to make some comments, which I have conveyed to Mr. Churchill.

It appears from the message that the date—February— fixed earlier for completing the operations in Tunisia is now set back to April. There is no need to demonstrate at length the undesirability of this delay in operations against the Germans and Italians. It is now, when the Soviet troops are still keeping up their broad offensive, that action by the Anglo-American troops in North Africa is imperative. Simultaneous pressure on Hitler from our front and from yours in Tunisia would be of great positive significance for our common cause and would create most serious difficulties for Hitler and Mussolini. It would also expedite the operations you are planning in Sicily and the Eastern Mediterranean.

As to the opening of a second front in Europe, in particular in France, it is planned, judging by your communication, for August or September. As I see it, however, the situation calls for shortening these time limits to the utmost and for the opening of a second front in the West at a date much earlier than the one mentioned. So that the enemy should not be given a chance to recover, it is very important, to my mind, that the blow from the West, instead of being put off till the second half of the year, be delivered in spring or early summer.

According to reliable information at our disposal, since the end of December, when for some reason the Anglo-American operations in Tunisia were suspended, the Germans have moved 27 divisions, including five armored divisions, to the Soviet-German front from France, the Low Countries, and Germany. In other words, instead of the Soviet Union being aided by diverting German forces from the Soviet-German front, what we get is relief for Hitler, who, because of the let-up in Anglo-American operations in Tunisia, was able to move additional troops against the Russians.

The foregoing indicates that the sooner we make joint use of the Hitler camps difficulties at the front, the more grounds we shall have for anticipating early defeat for Hitler. Unless we take account of this and profit by the present moment to further our common interests, it may well be that, having gained a respite and rallied their forces, the Germans might recover. It is clear to you and us that such an undesirable miscalculation should not be made.

FEBRUARY 16, 1943

F. Roosevelt to J. V. Stalin
Secret and Personal

In reply to your message of February 16 in which you set forth certain considerations that you had transmitted to Mr. Churchill in reply to his message of February 12 to you, I desire to state that I share your regret that the Allied effort in North Africa did not proceed in accordance with the schedule.

It was interrupted by unexpected heavy rains that made the roads extremely difficult for both supplies and troops proceeding to the front lines from our landing ports. These rains made the fields and mountains impassable.

I am fully aware of the adverse effect on the common Allied effort of this delay, and I am thinking [sic taking, Ed.] every possible step to begin successful aggressive action against the forces of the Axis in Africa at the earliest possible moment with the purpose of accomplishing their destruction.

The wide dispersion of America's transportation facilities at the present time is well known by you, and I can assure you that a maximum effort to increase our transportation is being made.

I understand the importance of a military effort on the continent of Europe at the earliest date practicable in order to reduce Axis resistance to your heroic army. You may be sure that the American war effort will be projected on to the European Continent at as early a date subsequent to success in North Africa as transportation facilities can be provided by our maximum effort.

We wish for the continuance of the success of your heroic army, which is an inspiration to all of us.

FEBRUARY 22, 1943

Sent on March 15, 1943

Personal and Secret Message
from Premier J. V. Stalin
to the Prime Minister,
Mr. W. Churchill

On March 12 Mr. Standley, the U.S. Ambassador, handed to Mr. Molotov the following message from the U.S. Government.

The U.S. Government offers to mediate between the U.S.S.R. and Finland with a view to ascertaining the possibility of a separate peace between them. Asked by Mr. Molotov whether the U.S. Government knew that Finland wanted peace and what her attitude was, Mr. Standley said he had nothing to say on the matter.

Most Secret and Personal Message from Premier J. V. Stalin to President Roosevelt

Now that I have Mr. Churchill's reply to my message of February 16, I consider it my duty to answer yours of February 22, which likewise was a reply to mine of February 16.

I learned from Mr. Churchill's message that Anglo-American operations in North Africa, far from being accelerated, are being postponed till the end of April; indeed, even this date is given in rather vague terms. In other words, at the height of the fighting against the Hitler troops—in February and March—the Anglo-American offensive in North Africa, far from having been stepped up, has been called off altogether, and the time fixed for it has been set back. Meanwhile Germany has succeeded in moving from the West 36 divisions, including six armored, to be used against the Soviet troops. The difficulties that this has created for the Soviet Army and the extent to which it has eased the German position on the Soviet-German front will be readily appreciated.

Mr. Churchill has also informed me that the Anglo-American operation against Sicily is planned for June. For all its importance, that operation can by no means replace a second front in France. But I fully welcome, of course, your intention to expedite the carrying out of the operation.

At the same time, I consider it my duty to state that the early opening of a second front in France is the most important thing. You will recall that you and Mr. Churchill thought it possible to open a second front as early as 1942 or this spring at the latest. The grounds for doing so were weighty enough. Hence it should be obvious why I stressed in my message of February 16 the need for striking in the West not later than this spring or early summer.

The Soviet troops have fought strenuously all winter and are continuing to do so, while Hitler is taking important measures to rehabilitate and reinforce his Army for the spring and summer operations against the U.S.S.R.; it is therefore particularly essential for us that the blow from the West be no longer delayed, that it be delivered this spring or in early summer.

I appreciate the considerable difficulties caused by a shortage of transport facilities, of which you advised me in your message. Nevertheless, I think I must give a most emphatic warning, in the interest of our common cause, of the grave danger with which further delay in opening a second front in France is fraught. That is why the vagueness of both your reply and Mr. Churchill's as to the opening of a second front in France causes me concern, which I cannot help expressing.

M A R C H 1 6 , 1 9 4 3

Personal and Secret Message from the Prime Minister, Mr. Winston Churchill, to Marshal Stalin

I am obliged to you for your telegram of March 15th about the American approach to you on the subject of Finland.

2. You can best judge how much military value it would be in the struggle against the Germans on your front to get

Finland out of the war. I should suppose it would have the effect of releasing more Soviet divisions than German divisions for use elsewhere. Further, the defection of Finland from the Axis might have a considerable effect on Hitler's other satellites.

3. The exclusion of the most clearly pro-German of the Finnish Ministers from the new government seems to have been a concession to public opinion and to denote a desire to show an independence of German control. It is thus possibly preparatory to a reorientation of Finnish policy when the moment is judged ripe. Although my own information, which is not very full, tends to show that the Finns are probably not yet ripe for negotiations, I feel that events on your front in the next few months will decide the issue for them. I believe them to be dependent on supplies of grain promised by the Germans for delivery between now and May. After these supplies have been received, Finland could probably get along without German food supplies until the end of the year.

4. Generally speaking, I should have thought that the Finns would be anxious to withdraw from the war as soon as they are convinced that Germany must be defeated. If so, it seems to me that it might not be altogether premature for you to ask the United States Government whether they know, or could find out without disclosing your interest, what terms the Finns would be prepared to accept. But you will be the best judge of the right tactics.

MARCH 20, 1943

Personal And Secret Operational Message from the Prime Minister, Mr. Winston Churchill, to Marshall J. V. Stalin

Our main battle in Tunisia is now in full swing. The American advance from the West began on March 17th. On the night of March 20th the Eighth Army attacked the fortifications of Mareth and is now driving through them in a north-westerly direction. At the same time, the New Zealand Army Corps with strong armored forces, by a circuitous march of over 150 miles, has reached a position behind the enemy about 30 miles west of Gabes. This Corps also reports progress towards the Gabes bottle-neck which is its objective. We have about 70,000 Germans and 50,000 Italians inside the closing circle, but it is too soon to speculate on what will happen. You will be able yourself to judge from the map the possibilities that are open. I will keep you informed.

2. Ten days of fog on our home landing grounds have held up our air offensive. It will begin again with added strength the moment the weather improves. I am sending you a few reels showing the destruction effected, particularly at Essen. I think you will like the look of these pictures as much as I do.

MARCH 23, 1943

Personal and Most Secret Message from the Prime Minister, Mr. Winston Churchill, to Marshal J. V. Stalin

The Germans have concentrated at Narvik a powerful battle fleet consisting of the *Tirpitz*, *Scharnhorst*, *Lutzow*, one 6-inch cruiser, and eight destroyers. Thus the danger to the Russian convoys which I described in my message to you of July 17th of last year has been revived in an even more menacing form. I told you then that we did not think it right to risk our Home Fleet in the Barents Sea, where it could be brought under the attack of German shore-based aircraft and U-boats without adequate protection against either, and I explained that if one or two of our most modern battleships were to be lost or even seriously damaged while the *Tirpitz* and other large units of the German battle fleet remained in action, the whole command of the Atlantic would be jeopardized with dire consequences to our common cause.

2. President Roosevelt and I have, therefore, decided with the greatest reluctance that it is impossible to provide adequate protection for the next Russian convoy and that without such protection there is not the slightest chance of any of the ships reaching you in the face of the known German preparations for their destruction. Orders have, therefore, been issued that the sailing of the March convoy is to be postponed.

3. It is a great disappointment to President Roosevelt and myself that it should be necessary to postpone the March convoy. Had it not been for the German concentration, it had been our firm intention to send you a convoy of thirty ships each in

March and again in early May. At the same time, we felt it only right to let you know at once that it will not be possible to continue convoys by the northern route after early May, since from that time onwards every single escort vessel will be required to support our offensive operations in the Mediterranean, leaving only a minimum to safeguard our lifelines in the Atlantic. In the latter, we have had grievous and almost unprecedented losses during the last three weeks. Assuming that "Husky" goes well, we should hope to resume convoys in early September, provided that the disposition of German main units permits and that the situation in the North Atlantic is such as to enable us to provide the necessary escorts and covering force.

4. We are doing our utmost to increase the flow of supplies by the southern route. The monthly figure has been more than doubled in the last six months. We have reason to hope that the increase will be progressive and that the figures for August will reach 240,000 tons. If this is achieved, the month's delivery will have increased eightfold in twelve months. Furthermore, the United States will materially increase shipments via Vladivostok. This will in some way offset both your disappointment and ours at the interruption to the northern convoys.

MARCH 30, 1943

Personal and Secret Message from Premier J. V. Stalin to the Prime Minister, Mr. W. Churchill

The behavior of the Polish Government towards the U.S.S.R. of late is, in the view of the Soviet Government, completely abnormal and contrary to all the rules and standards governing relations between two allied states.

The anti-Soviet slander campaign launched by the German fascists in connection with the Polish officers whom they themselves murdered in the Smolensk area, in German-occupied territory, was immediately seized upon by the Sikorski Government and is being fanned in every way by the Polish official press. Far from countering the infamous fascist slander against the U.S.S.R., the Sikorski Government has not found it necessary even to address questions to the Soviet Government or to request information on the matter.

The Hitler authorities, having perpetrated a monstrous crime against the Polish officers, are now staging a farcical investigation, using for the purpose certain profascist Polish elements picked by themselves in occupied Poland, where everything is under Hitler's heel and where no honest Pole can open his mouth.

Both the Sikorski and Hitler Governments have enlisted for the "investigation" the aid of the International Red Cross, which, under a terror régime of gallows and wholesale extermination of the civil population, is forced to take part in the investigation farce directed by Hitler. It is obvious that this "investigation," which, moreover, is being carried out behind the Soviet Government's back, cannot enjoy the confidence of anyone with a semblance of honesty.

The fact that the anti-Soviet campaign has been started simultaneously in the German and Polish press and follows identical lines is indubitable evidence of contact and collusion between Hitler—the Allies' enemy—and the Sikorski Government in this hostile campaign.

At a time when the peoples of the Soviet Union are shedding their blood in a grim struggle against Hitler Germany and bending their energies to defeat the common foe of the freedom-loving democratic countries, the Sikorski Government is striking a treacherous blow at the Soviet Union to help Hitler tyranny.

These circumstances compel the Soviet Government to consider that the present Polish Government, having descended to collusion with the Hitler Government, has, in practice, severed its relations of alliance with the U.S.S.R. and adopted a hostile attitude to the Soviet Union.

For these reasons, the Soviet Government has decided to interrupt relations with that Government.

I think it necessary to inform you of the foregoing, and I trust that the British Government will appreciate the motives that necessitated this forced step on the part of the Soviet Government.

APRIL 21, 1943

Personal and Secret Message
from the Prime Minister,
Mr. Winston Churchill,
to Marshal J. V. Stalin

Ambassador Maisky delivered your message to me last
night. We shall certainly oppose vigorously any "investigation" by the International Red Cross or any other body in any
territory under German authority. Such investigation would be
a fraud, and its conclusions reached by terrorism. Mr. Eden is
seeing Sikorski today and will press him as strongly as possible to withdraw all countenance from any investigation under
Nazi auspices. Also we should never approve of any parley
with the Germans or contact with them of any kind whatever
and we shall press this point upon our Polish allies.

2. I shall telegraph to you later how Sikorski reacts to the
above points. His position is one of great difficulty. Far from
being pro-German or in league with them, he is in danger of
being overthrown by the Poles who consider that he has not
stood up sufficiently for his people against the Soviets. If he
should go, we should only get somebody worse. I hope therefore that your decision to "interrupt" relations is to be read in
the sense of a final warning rather than of a break and that it
will not be made public at any rate until every other plan has
been tried. The public announcement of a break would do the
greatest possible harm in the United States, where the Poles
are numerous and influential.

3. I had drafted a telegram to you yesterday asking you to
consider allowing more Poles and Polish dependents to go into
Iran. This would allay the rising discontent of the Polish Army
formed there and would enable me to influence the Polish

Government to act in conformity with our common interests and against the common foe. I have deferred sending this telegram in consequence of yours to me in hopes that the situation may clear.

APRIL 24, 1943

Personal and Secret Message from Premier Stalin to the Prime Minister, Mr. W. Churchill

I have received your message concerning Polish affairs. Thank you for your sympathetic stand on this issue. I must tell you, however, that the matter of interrupting relations with the Polish Government has already been settled and that today V. M. Molotov delivered a Note to the Polish Government. All my colleagues insisted on this because the Polish official press is not only keeping up its hostile campaign but is actually intensifying it day by day. I also had to take cognizance of Soviet public opinion, which is deeply outraged by the ingratitude and treachery of the Polish Government.

As to publishing the Soviet document on interrupting relations with the Polish Government, I fear that it is simply impossible to avoid doing so.

APRIL 25, 1943

Personal and Secret Message from the President to Mr. Stalin

I received your telegram during an inspection trip which I was making in the western part of the United States. I fully understand your problem, but at the same time I hope that you can find a way in this present situation to define your action as a suspension of conversations with the Polish Government in exile in London, rather than to label it as a complete severance of diplomatic relations between the Soviet Union and Poland.

I cannot believe that Sikorski has in any way whatsoever collaborated with the Hitler gangsters. In my opinion, however, he has erred in taking up this particular question with the International Red Cross. Furthermore, I am inclined to think that Prime Minister Churchill will find a way of prevailing upon the Polish Government in London in the future to act with more common sense.

I would appreciate it if you would let me know if I can help in any way in respect to this question and particularly in connection with looking after any Poles which [sic] you may desire to send out of the Union of Soviet Socialist Republics.

Incidentally, I have several million Poles in the United States, a great many of whom are in the Army and Navy. I can assure you that all of them are bitter against the Hitlerites. However, the overall situation would not be helped by the knowledge of a complete diplomatic break between the Soviet and Polish Governments.

APRIL 26, 1943

Personal and Secret Message from Premier J. V. Stalin to the President, Mr. Franklin D. Roosevelt

I am sorry to say your reply did not reach me until April 27, whereas on April 25 the Soviet Government was compelled to interrupt relations with the Polish Government.

As the Polish Government for nearly two weeks, far from ceasing a campaign hostile to the Soviet Union and beneficial to none but Hitler, intensified it in its press and on the radio, Soviet public opinion was deeply outraged by such conduct, and hence the Soviet Government could no longer defer action.

It may well be that Mr. Sikorski himself has no intention of collaborating with the Hitler gangsters. I should be happy to see this surmise borne out by facts. But my impression is that certain pro-Hitler elements—either inside the Polish Government or in its environment—have induced Mr. Sikorski to follow them, with the result that the Polish Government has come to be, possibly against its own will, a tool in Hitler's hands in the anti-Soviet campaign of which you are aware.

I, too, believe that Prime Minister Churchill will find ways to bring the Polish Government to reason and help it proceed henceforward in a spirit of common sense. I may be wrong, but I believe that one of our duties as Allies is to prevent this or that Ally from taking hostile action against any other Ally to the joy and benefit of the common enemy.

As regards Polish subjects in the U.S.S.R. and their future, I can assure you that Soviet Government agencies have always treated and will continue to treat them as comrades, as people

near and dear to us. It should be obvious that there never has
been, nor could have been, any question of their being de-
ported from the U.S.S.R. If, however, they themselves wish
to leave the U.S.S.R., Soviet Government agencies will not
hinder them, just as they have never done, and will, in fact,
try to help them.

APRIL 29, 1943

Personal and Secret Message
from the Prime Minister,
Mr. Winston Churchill,
to Marshal J. V. Stalin

I cannot refrain from expressing my disappointment that
you should have felt it necessary to take action in breaking off
relations with the Poles without giving me time to inform you
of the results of my approach to General Sikorski, about
which I had telegraphed to you on April 24th. I had hoped
that, in the spirit of our treaty of last year, we should always
consult each other about such important matters, more especially as they affect the combined strength of the United
Nations.

2. Mr. Eden and I have pointed out to the Polish Government that no resumption of friendly or working relations with
the Soviets is possible while they make charges of an insulting
character against the Soviet Government and thus seem to

countenance the atrocious Nazi propaganda. Still more would it be impossible for any of us to tolerate inquiries by the International Red Cross held under Nazi auspices and dominated by Nazi terrorism. I am glad to tell you that they have accepted our view and that they want to work loyally with you. Their request now is to have dependents of the Polish Army in Iran and the fighting Poles in the Soviet Union sent to join the Polish forces already allowed to go to Iran. This is surely a matter which admits of patient discussion. We think the request is reasonable if made in the right way and at the right time, and I am pretty sure that the President thinks so, too. We hope earnestly that remembering the difficulties in which we have all been plunged by the brutal Nazi aggression, you will consider this matter in a spirit of collaboration.

3. The Cabinet here is determined to have proper discipline in the Polish press in Great Britain. The miserable rags attacking Sikorski can say things which German broadcasts repeat openmouthed to the world to our joint detriment. This must be stopped and it will be stopped.

4. So far this business has been Goebbels' triumph. He is now busy suggesting that the U.S.S.R. will set up a Polish Government on Russian soil and deal only with them. We should not, of course, be able to recognize such a Government and would continue our relations with Sikorski, who is far the most helpful man you or we are likely to find for the purposes of the common cause. I expect that this will also be the American view.

5. My own feeling is that they have had a shock and that after whatever interval is thought convenient the relationship established on July 30th, 1941 should be restored. No one will hate this more than Hitler, and what he hates most is wise for us to do.

6. We owe it to our armies now engaged and presently to be more heavily engaged to maintain good conditions behind the fronts. I and my colleagues look steadily to the ever closer cooperation and understanding of the U.S.S.R., the United States and the British Commonwealth and Empire, not only in the deepening war struggle, but after the war. What other hope can there be than this for the tortured world?

APRIL 30, 1943

Personal and Secret Message from Premier J. V. Stalin to the Prime Minister, Mr. W. Churchill

In sending my message of April 21 on interrupting relations with the Polish Government, I was guided by the fact that the notorious anti-Soviet press campaign, launched by the Poles as early as April 15 and aggravated first by the statement of the Polish Ministry of National Defense and later by the Polish Government's declaration of April 17, had not encountered any opposition in London; moreover, the Soviet Government had not been forewarned of the anti-Soviet campaign prepared by the Poles, although it is hard to imagine that the British Government was not informed of the contemplated campaign. I think that from the point of view of the spirit of our treaty, it would have been only natural to dissuade one ally from striking a blow at another, particularly if the blow directly helped the common enemy. That, at any rate, is how I see the duty of an ally. Nevertheless, I thought it necessary to inform you of the Soviet Government's view of Polish-Soviet relations. Since the Poles continued their anti-Soviet smear campaign without any opposition in London, the patience of the Soviet Government could not have been expected to be infinite.

You tell me that you will enforce proper discipline in the Polish press. I thank you for that, but I doubt if it will be as easy as all that to impose discipline on the present Polish Government, its following of pro-Hitler boosters and its fanatical press. Although you informed me that the Polish Government wanted to work loyally with the Soviet Government, I question its ability to keep its word. The Polish Government is surrounded by such a vast pro-Hitler following, and Sikorski is so helpless and browbeaten that there is no certainty at all of his being able to remain loyal in relations with the Soviet Union even granting that he wants to be loyal.

As to the rumors, circulated by the Hitlerites, that a new Polish Government is being formed in the U.S.S.R., there is hardly any need to deny this fabrication. Our Ambassador has already told you so. This does not rule out Great Britain, and the U.S.S.R. and the U.S.A. taking measures to improve the composition of the present Polish Government in terms of consolidating the Allied united front against Hitler. The sooner this is done, the better. Upon his return from the U.S.A., Mr. Eden told Maisky that President Roosevelt's adherents in the U.S.A. thought that the present Polish Government had no prospects for the future and doubted whether it had any chance of returning to Poland and assuming power, although they would like to retain Sikorski. I think the Americans are not so very far from the truth as regards the prospects of the present Polish Government.

As regards the Polish citizens in the U.S.S.R., whose number is not great, and the families of the Polish soldiers evacuated to Iran, the Soviet Government has never raised any obstacles to their departure from the U.S.S.R.

2. I have received your message on the latest events in Tunisia. Thank you for the information. I am glad of the success of the Anglo-American troops and wish them still greater success.

MAY 4, 1943

J. V. Stalin to F. Roosevelt

My dear Mr. Roosevelt,

Mr. Davies has delivered your message to me.

I agree that this summer—possibly as early as June—we should expect the Hitlerites to launch a new major offensive on the Soviet-German front. Hitler has already concentrated about 200 German divisions and up to 30 divisions of his allies for use against us. We are getting ready to repel the new German offensive and to launch counterattacks, but we are short of aircraft and aircraft fuel. Of course, it is at the moment impossible to foresee all the military and other steps that we may have to take. That will depend on the course of events on our front. A good deal will also depend on the speed and vigor with which Anglo-American military operations are launched in Europe.

I have mentioned these important circumstances to explain why my reply to your suggestion for a meeting between us cannot be quite specific as yet.

I agree that the time is ripe for such a meeting and that it should not be delayed. But I beg you to assess properly the importance of the circumstances I have referred to, because the summer months will be exceedingly trying for the Soviet armies. As I do not know how events will develop on the Soviet-German front in June, I shall not be able to leave Moscow during that month. I therefore suggest holding the meeting in July or August. If you agree, I shall let you know two weeks before the date of the meeting just when it could be held in July or August. If, after being notified by me, you agree to the date suggested, I could arrive in time.

Mr. Davies will personally inform you of the meeting place.

I agree with you about cutting down the number of your advisers and mine.

Thank you for sending Mr. Davies to Moscow, a man familiar with the Soviet Union and who can pass impartial judgment on things.

Yours very sincerely,
J. STALIN

MAY 26, 1943

Received on June 4, 1943

From President Roosevelt to Mr. Stalin (Personal and Most Secret)

Basic strategy in the recent decisions approved by the Combined Chiefs of Staff is divided into the below-listed groupings:

A. The control of the threat developed by enemy submarines receives primary consideration, along with the security of Allied maritime communication lines and with every practicable means of support for the Soviet Union.

B. The laying of preparatory groundwork for the participation of Turkey in the war, either as an active or as a passive ally.

C. The reduction of Japanese military power by keeping up an unremitting pressure against her.

D. The carrying out of those measures found practicable by which China may be kept in the war as an effective power and maintained as a base from which operations may be carried out against Japan.

E. The rendering of such aid and assistance to the French forces in Africa that they may be prepared for an active part in the attacks to be made on enemy-held territory in Europe.

Referring to (A) above, we have been greatly encouraged by results recently obtained against enemy submarines by the use of long-range airplanes carrying new devices and equipment and also of groups of special attack vessels. Since the first of May, we have destroyed an average of more than one submarine per day. Destruction at this rate over a period of time will have a tremendous effect on the morale of the crews of the German undersea fleet. It will eventually reduce our ship losses and will thereby increase our shipping pool.

In respect support of the U.S.S.R., the following decisions were made: the air offensive now being mounted against enemy-held Europe will be intensified, for the threefold purpose of destruction of enemy industry, of whittling down of German fighter-plane strength, and for the breaking of German civil morale. That this intensification is already in progress is demonstrated by the events of the last three weeks, during which France, Italy, Germany, Sicily, and Sardinia have been heavily attacked. British strength in Bomber Command is growing steadily. The United States heavy bomber force operating in England has increased at a constant rate and will continue to do so. In March, there were about 350 United States heavy bombers in England. At the present time there are about 700. Plans call for 900 at the end of June, 1,150 at the end of September and 2,500 by the first of April.

It has been decided to put Italy out of the war at the earliest possible moment. The plan for the attack on Sicily is designated as "Husky." General Eisenhower has been ordered that when "Husky" has been successfully concluded, he is to be prepared to immediately launch offensives directed toward the collapse of Italy. Forces available to Eisenhower for these operations will be the total now in the Mediterranean theater less four American and three British divisions which are to be sent to England as part of a concentration of forces in that country shortly to be referred to below.

The collapse of Italy will greatly facilitate the carrying out of the air offensive against South and East Germany, will continue the attrition of their fighter strength and will jeopardize the Axis position in the Balkan area.

With Africa firmly in our hands, it was decided that it was now feasible to resume the concentration of ground forces in England. A joint Anglo-American staff has been and is constantly occupied with keeping up to the last minute the necessary plans for instantly taking advantage of any enemy weakness in France or Norway. Under the present plans, there should be a sufficiently large concentration of men and matériel in the British Isles in the spring of 1944 to permit a full-scale invasion of the continent at that time. The great air offensive will then be at its peak. A certain number of large landing craft have necessarily been sent to the Southwest Pacific, the Aleutians, and to the Mediterranean. The necessity of so doing has of course reduced by that extent the number of such boats sent to England. This has been the most important limiting factor as far as operations out of England have been concerned.

The decisions enumerated and explained above are believed to be such that the enemy will be forced to disperse his ground forces to an excessive degree, both to oppose actual attacks and to guard against the possibility of attack. He will in addition be subject to heavy and continuous activity in the air. When signs of Axis weakness become apparent in any quarter, actual attacks and threats of attack will easily and quickly be translated into successful operations. We believe that these decisions as stated herein will require the full resources which we will be able to bring to bear.

ROOSEVELT

Sent on June 11, 1943

Personal and Secret Message from Premier J. V. Stalin to the President, Mr. Roosevelt

Your message informing me of certain decisions on strategic matters adopted by you and Mr. Churchill reached me on June 4. Thank you for the information.

It appears from your communication that the decisions run counter to those reached by you and Mr. Churchill earlier this year concerning the date for a second front in Western Europe.

You will doubtless recall that the joint message of January 26, sent by you and Mr. Churchill, announced the decision adopted at that time to divert considerable German ground and air forces from the Russian front and bring Germany to her knees in 1943.

Then, on February 12, Mr. Churchill communicated on his own behalf and yours the specified time of the Anglo-American operation in Tunisia and the Mediterranean, as well as on the west coast of Europe. The communication said that Great Britain and the United States were vigorously preparing to cross the Channel in August 1943, and that if the operation were hindered by weather or other causes, then it would be prepared with an eye to being carried out in greater force in September 1943.

Now, in May 1943, you and Mr. Churchill have decided to postpone the Anglo-American invasion of Western Europe until the spring of 1944. In other words, the opening of the second front in Western Europe, previously postponed from

1942 till 1943, is now being put off again, this time till the spring of 1944.

Your decision creates exceptional difficulties for the Soviet Union, which, straining all its resources, for the past two years, has been engaged against the main forces of Germany and her satellites, and leaves the Soviet Army, which is fighting not only for its country, but for its Allies, to do the job alone almost single-handed, against an enemy that is still very strong and formidable.

Need I speak of the disheartening negative impression that this fresh postponement of the second front and the withholding from our Army, which has sacrificed so much, of the anticipated substantial support by the Anglo-American armies, will produce in the Soviet Union—both among the people and in the Army?

As for the Soviet Government, it cannot align itself with this decision, which, moreover, was adopted without its participation and without any attempt at a joint discussion of this highly important matter and which may gravely affect the subsequent course of the war.

Received on June 22, 1943

Marshal Joseph V. Stalin, Commander-in-Chief of the Armed Forces of the U.S.S.R.

The Kremlin, Moscow

Two years ago tomorrow, by an act of treachery in keeping with the long record of Nazi duplicity, the Nazi leaders launched their brutal attack upon the Soviet Union. They thus added to their growing list of enemies the mighty forces of the Soviet Union. These Nazi leaders had underestimated the extent to which the Soviet Government and people had developed and strengthened their military power to defend their country and had utterly failed to realize the determination and valor of the Soviet people during the past two years. The freedom-loving peoples of the world have watched with increasing admiration the history-making exploits of the armed forces of the Soviet Union and the almost incredible sacrifices which the Russian people are so heroically making. The growing might of the combined forces of all the United Nations which is being brought increasingly to bear upon our common enemy testifies to the spirit of unity and sacrifice necessary for our ultimate victory. This same spirit will, I am sure, animate us in approaching the challenging tasks of peace, which victory will present to the world.

Franklin D. ROOSEVELT

Personal and Secret Message from Premier J. V. Stalin to the President, Mr. Roosevelt

I am sending you the text of my reply to a message from Mr. Churchill, with which you are in full accord, as stated in the message delivered to me by Mr. Standley on June 20.

JUNE 24, 1943

Personal and Secret Message from Premier J. V. Stalin to the Prime Minister, Mr. W. Churchill

Your message of June 19 received.

I fully realize the difficulty of organizing an Anglo-American invasion of Western Europe, in particular, of transferring troops across the Channel. The difficulty could also be discerned in your communications.

From your messages of last year and this, I gained the conviction that you and the President were fully aware of the difficulties of organizing such an operation and were preparing the invasion accordingly, with due regard to the difficulties and the necessary exertion of forces and means. Even last year you told me that a large-scale invasion of Europe by Anglo-American troops would be effected in 1943. In the Aide-Mémoire handed to V. M. Molotov on June 10, 1942, you wrote:

"Finally, and most important of all, we are concentrating our maximum effort on the organisation and preparation of a large-scale invasion of the Continent of Europe by British and American forces in 1943. We are setting no limit to the scope and objectives of this campaign, which will be carried out in the first instance by over a million men, British and American, with air forces of appropriate strength."

Early this year you twice informed me, on your own behalf and on behalf of the President, of decisions concerning an Anglo-American invasion of Western Europe intended to "divert strong German land and air forces from the Russian front." You had set yourself the task of bringing Germany to her knees as early as 1943, and named September as the latest date for the invasion.

In your message of January 26 you wrote:

"We have been in conference with our military advisers and have decided on the operations which are to be undertaken by the American and British forces in the first nine months of 1943. We wish to inform you of our intentions at once. We believe that these operations together with your powerful offensive, may well bring Germany to her knees in 1943."

In your next message, which I received on February 12, you wrote, specifying the date of the invasion of Western Europe, decided on by you and the President:

"We are also pushing preparations to the limit of our resources for a cross-Channel operation in August, in which British and United States units would participate. Here again, shipping and assault-landing craft will be the limiting factors. If the operation is delayed by the weather or other reasons, it will be prepared with stronger forces for September."

Last February, when you wrote to me about those plans and the date for invading Western Europe, the difficulties of that operation were greater than they are now. Since then the Germans have suffered more than one defeat: they were pushed back by our troops in the South, where they suffered appreciable loss; they were beaten in North Africa and expelled by the Anglo-American troops; in submarine warfare, too, the Germans found themselves in a bigger predicament than ever, while Anglo-American superiority increased substantially; it is also known that the Americans and British have won air superiority in Europe and that their navies and mercantile marines have grown in power.

It follows that the conditions for opening a second front in Western Europe during 1943, far from deteriorating, have, indeed, greatly improved.

That being so, the Soviet Government could not have imagined that the British and U.S. Governments would revise the decision to invade Western Europe, which they had adopted early this year. In fact, the Soviet Government was fully entitled to expect that the Anglo-American decision would be carried out, that appropriate preparations were under way and that the second front in Western Europe would at last be opened in 1943.

That is why, when you now write that "it would be no help to Russia if we threw away a hundred thousand men in a disastrous cross-Channel attack," all I can do is remind you of the following:

First, your own Aide-Mémoire of June 1942 in which you declared that preparations were under way for an invasion, not by a hundred thousand, but by an Anglo-American force exceeding one million men at the very start of the operation.

Second, your February message, which mentioned extensive measures preparatory to the invasion of Western Europe in August or September 1943, which, apparently, envisaged an operation, not by a hundred thousand men, but by an adequate force.

So when you now declare: "I cannot see how a great British defeat and slaughter would aid the Soviet armies," is it not clear that a statement of this kind in relation to the Soviet Union is utterly groundless and directly contradicts your previous and responsible decisions, listed above, about extensive and vigorous measures by the British and Americans to organize the invasion this year, measures on which the complete success of the operation should hinge.

I shall not enlarge on the fact that this responsible decision, revoking your previous decisions on the invasion of Western Europe, was reached by you and the President without Soviet participation and without inviting its representatives to the Washington conference, although you cannot but be aware that the Soviet Union's role in the war against Germany and its interest in the problems of the second front are great enough.

You say that you "quite understand" my disappointment. I must tell you that the point here is not just the disappointment of the Soviet Government, but the preservation of its confidence in its Allies, a confidence which is being subjected to severe stress. One should not forget that it is a question of saving millions of lives in the occupied areas of Western Europe and Russia and of reducing the enormous sacrifices of the Soviet armies, compared with which the sacrifices of the Anglo-American armies are insignificant.

JUNE 24, 1943

Personal and Most Secret Message
from the Prime Minister,
Mr. Winston Churchill,
to Marshal J. V. Stalin

I am concerned to hear, through Monsieur Molotov, that
you are thinking of recognizing the French National Committee of Liberation recently set up at Algiers. It is unlikely that
the British, and still more that the United States Government,
will recognize this Committee for some time, and then only
after they have had reasonable proof that its character and
action will be satisfactory to the interests of the Allied cause.

2. Since he arrived at Algiers, General de Gaulle has been
struggling to obtain effective control of the French Army.
Headquarters cannot be sure of what he will do or of his
friendly feelings towards us if he obtained the mastery. President Roosevelt and I are in entire agreement in feeling that de
Gaulle might endanger the base and communications of the
armies about to operate in Husky. We cannot run any risk of
this, as it would affect the lives of our soldiers and hamper the
prosecution of the war.

3. Originally there were seven members of the Committee
but the number has now been expanded to fourteen, and we
cannot be sure of its action. General Eisenhower has, therefore, in the name of both the United States and the British
Governments, notified the Committee that General Giraud
must remain the Commander-in-Chief of the French Army and
have effective power over its character and organization. Undoubtedly this will cause discussion in the House of Commons
as well as in the United States, and the President and I will
have to give reasons, of which there are plenty, for the course

we have taken. If the Soviet Government had already recognized the Committee the mere giving of these reasons and the explanations would reveal a difference of view between the Soviet Government and the Western Allies, which would be most regrettable.

4. We are very anxious to find a French authority to which all Frenchmen will rally, and we still hope that one may emerge from the discussions now proceeding at Algiers. It seems to us far too soon to decide upon this at present.

JUNE 23, 1943

Personal and Secret Message
from the Prime Minister,
Mr. Winston Churchill,
to Marshal J. V. Stalin

Mr. Eden saw General Sikorski yesterday evening. Sikorski stated that so far from synchronizing his appeal to the Red Cross with that of the Germans, his Government took the initiative without knowing what line the Germans would take. In fact, the Germans acted after hearing the Polish broadcast announcement. Sikorski also told Mr. Eden that his Government had simultaneously approached Monsieur Bogomolov on the subject. Sikorski emphasized that previously he had several times raised this question of the missing officers with the Soviet Government and once with you personally. On his instructions, the Polish Minister of Information in his broadcasts has reacted strongly against the German propaganda and this has brought an angry German reply. As a result of Mr. Eden's strong representations, Sikorski has undertaken not to press the request for the Red Cross investigation and will so inform the Red Cross authorities in Berne. He will also restrain the Polish press from polemics. In this connection, I am examining the possibility of silencing those Polish newspapers in this country which attacked the Soviet Government and at the same time attacked Sikorski for trying to work with the Soviet Government.

In view of Sikorski's undertaking, I would now urge you to abandon the idea of any interruption of relations.

I have reflected further on this matter, and I am more than ever convinced that it can only assist our enemies, if there is a break between the Soviet and Polish Governments. German propaganda has produced this story precisely in order to make a rift in the ranks of the United Nations and to lend some semblance of reality to its new attempts to persuade the world that the interests of Europe and the smaller nations are being defended by Germany against the great extra-European Powers, namely the Union of Soviet Socialist Republics, the United States, and the British Empire.

I know General Sikorski well, and I am convinced that no contacts or understanding could exist between him or his Government and our common enemy, against whom he has led the Poles in bitter and uncompromising resistance. His appeal to the International Red Cross was clearly a mistake, though I am convinced that it was not made in collusion with the Germans.

Now that we have, I hope, cleared up the issue raised in your telegram to me, I want to revert to the proposals contained in my draft telegram to which I referred in my message of April 24th. I shall therefore shortly be sending you this earlier message in its original form. If we two were able to arrange to link the matter of getting these Poles out of the Soviet Union, it would be easier for Sikorski to withdraw entirely from the position he has been forced by his public opinion to adopt. I hope that you will help me to achieve this.

APRIL 25, 1943

Personal and Secret Message from Premier J. V. Stalin to the Prime Minister, Mr. Winston Churchill

I have received your message of June 23, 1943, in which you point out that for the present the Governments of Great Britain and the United States of America will refrain from recognizing the French National Committee of Liberation. In support of your attitude, you say that Headquarters cannot be sure what action General de Gaulle may undertake or of his friendly feelings for the Allies.

We had the impression that the British Government had thus far supported General de Gaulle, which seemed only natural, since from the moment of the French surrender General de Gaulle had headed the anti-Hitler forces of France and the struggle of the French patriots united around Fighting France. Subsequent developments in North Africa, beginning with November 1942, and the part played by French armed forces under Generals Giraud and de Gaulle in the operations carried out by the Anglo-American troops provided the conditions for their union. All the Allies concurred that this union was advisable, and there were no doubts as to this point. Recognition of the existing united agency in the form of the French National Committee of Liberation was to be a result of the aspirations displayed and the efforts made in this matter. All the more so because, after the French National Committee in the persons of Giraud and de Gaulle officially requested Allied recognition of the Committee, the Soviet Government felt that refusal to grant the request would be incomprehensible to French public opinion.

At the moment the Soviet Government has no information that could support the British Government's present attitude to the French National Committee of Liberation and, in particular, to General de Gaulle.

Since, however, the British Government requests that the recognition of the French Committee be postponed and through its Ambassador has given the assurance that no steps will be taken in this matter without consulting the Soviet Government, the Soviet Government is prepared to meet the British Government halfway.

I hope you will take cognizance of the Soviet interest in French affairs and not deny the Soviet Government timely information, which is indispensable for the adoption of appropriate decisions.

J U N E 2 6 , 1 9 4 3

Secret and Personal Message from Premier J. V. Stalin to President Franklin D. Roosevelt

I can answer your latest message—that of July 16—now that I am back from the front. I have no doubt that you are aware of our military position and will appreciate the delay.

Contrary to our expectations, the Germans launched their offensive in July, not in June, and now fighting is in full swing on the Soviet-German front. The Soviet armies have, as you know, repulsed the July offensive of the Hitlerites, switched to the offensive, taking Orel and Belgorod, and are still pressing the enemy.

It will be readily seen that in the present crucial situation on the Soviet-German front the Soviet Command has to exert great efforts and display the utmost vigilance towards the enemy's activities. For this reason I, too, am compelled to put aside other problems and my other duties, to a certain degree, except my chief duty, that of directing the front. I have to go to the various front sectors more frequently and to subordinate all else to the interests of the front.

I hope you will appreciate that in these circumstances I cannot start on a distant journey and shall unfortunately be unable during the summer and autumn to make good the promise I gave you through Mr. Davies.

I am very sorry about this, but circumstances, as you know, are stronger than people, and so we must bow to them.

I consider it highly advisable for responsible representatives of our two countries to meet. In the present military situation, the meeting could be held either in Astrakhan or in Archangel. If that does not suit you personally, then you might send a fully authorized man of confidence to one of these two towns. If you accept, we should specify beforehand the range of problems to be discussed at the conference and draft appropriate proposals.

I have already told Mr. Davies that I have no objection to Mr. Churchill attending the conference and to the bipartite conference being turned into a tripartite one. I still hold this view provided you have no objections.

2. I take this opportunity to congratulate you and the Anglo-American forces on their outstanding success in Sicily, which has led to the fall of Mussolini and his gang.

3. Thank you for congratulating the Red Army and the Soviet people on their success at Orel.

AUGUST 8, 1943

Most Secret and Personal Message from President Roosevelt and the Prime Minister, Mr. Winston Churchill, to Marshal J. V. Stalin

On August 15th the British Ambassador at Madrid reported that General Castellano had arrived from Badoglio with a letter of introduction from the British Minister to the Vatican. The General declared that he was authorized by Badoglio to say that Italy was willing to surrender unconditionally provided that she could join the Allies. The British representative to the Vatican has since been furnished by Marshal Badoglio with a written statement that he has duly authorized General Castellano. This therefore seems a firm offer.

We are not prepared to enter into any bargain with Badoglio's Government to induce Italy to change sides; on the other hand, there are many advantages and a great speeding-up of the campaign which might follow there-from. We shall begin our invasion of the mainland of Italy probably before the end of this month, and about a week later we shall make our full-scale thrust at "Avalanche." It is very likely that Badoglio's Government will not last so long. The Germans have one or more armored division outside Rome, and once they think that the Badoglio Government is playing them false, they are quite capable of overthrowing it and setting up a Quisling Government of Fascist elements under, for instance, Farinacci. Alternatively, Badoglio may collapse and the whole of Italy pass into disorder.

Such being the situation, the Combined Chiefs of Staff

have prepared, and the President and the Prime Minister approved, as a measure of military diplomacy, the following instructions which have been sent to General Eisenhower for action:

"The President and the Prime Minister having approved, the Combined Chiefs of Staff direct you to send at once to Lisbon two Staff Officers; one United States', and one British. They should report upon arrival to the British Ambassador. They should take with them agreed armistice terms which have already been sent to you. Acting on instructions, the British Ambassador at Lisbon will have arranged a meeting with General Castellano. Your Staff Officers will be present at this meeting.

At this meeting a communication to General Castellano will be made on the following lines:

(a) The unconditional surrender of Italy is accepted on the terms stated in the document to be handed to him. (He should then be given the armistice terms for Italy already agreed and previously sent to you. He should be told that these do *not* include the political, economic or financial terms which will be communicated later by other means.)

(b) These terms do *not* visualize active assistance of Italy in fighting the Germans. The extent to which the terms will be modified in favor of Italy will depend on how far the Italian Government and people do, in fact, aid the United Nations against Germany during the remainder of the war. The United Nations, however, state without reservation, that wherever Italian troops or Italians fight the Germans, or destroy German property, or hamper German movements, they will be given all possible support by troops of the United Nations. Meanwhile, provided that information about the enemy is immediately and regularly supplied, Allied bombing will so far as possible be directed on targets which affect the movements and operations of German troops.

(c) Cessation of hostilities between the United Nations and Italy will take effect from a date and hour to be notified by General Eisenhower.

(Note: General Eisenhower should make this notification a few hours before Allied troops land in Italy in strength.)

(d) Italian Government must undertake to proclaim the

Armistice immediately it is announced by General Eisenhower, and to order their troops and people from that hour to collaborate with the Allies and to resist the Germans.

(Note: As will be seen from 2(c) above, the Italian Government will be given a few hours' notice.)

(e) Italian Government must, at the hour of Armistice, order that all United Nations prisoners in danger of capture by the Germans shall be immediately released.

(f) Italian Government must, at the hour of Armistice, order the Italian fleet and as much of their merchant shipping as possible to put to sea for Allied ports. As many military aircraft as possible shall fly to Allied bases. Any ships or aircraft in danger of capture must be destroyed.

2. General Castellano should be told that meanwhile there is a good deal that Badoglio can do without the Germans becoming aware of what is afoot. The precise character and extent of his action must be left to his judgment but the following are the general lines which should be suggested to him:

(a) General passive resistance throughout the country if this order can be conveyed to local authorities without the Germans' knowing.

(b) Minor sabotage throughout the country, particularly of communications and of air fields used by the Germans.

(c) Safeguard of Allied prisoners of war. If German pressure to hand them over becomes too great, they should be released.

(d) *No* Italian warships to be allowed to fall into German hands. Arrangements to be made to ensure that all of these ships can sail to ports designated by General Eisenhower immediately he gives the order. Italian submarines should *not* be withdrawn from patrol as this would reveal our common purpose to the enemy.

(e) *No* merchant shipping to be allowed to fall into German hands. Merchant shipping in northern ports should, if possible, be sailed to ports south of a line Venice-Leghorn. In the last resort, they should be scuttled. All ships must be ready to sail for ports designated by General Eisenhower.

(f) Germans must not be allowed to take over Italian coast defenses.

(g) Instructions to be put into force at the proper time

for Italian formations in the Balkans to march to the coast with a view to their being taken off to Italy by the United Nations.

3. A safe channel of communication between General Eisenhower and the Italian headquarters is to be arranged with General Castellano by General Eisenhower's representatives."

(End of General Eisenhower's message.)

To turn to another subject, following on decisions taken at "Trident." His Majesty's Government entered upon negotiations with Portugal in order to obtain naval and air facilities in a "life-belt." Accordingly, His Majesty's Ambassador at Lisbon invoked the Anglo-Portuguese Alliance which has lasted 600 years unbroken and invited Portugal to grant the said facilities. Dr. Salazar was, of course, oppressed by the fear of German bombing out of revenge and of possible hostile moves by the Spaniards. We have accordingly furnished him with supplies of anti-aircraft artillery and fighter aircraft which are now in transit, and we have also informed Dr. Salazar that should Spain attack Portugal, we shall immediately declare war on Spain and render such help as is in our power. We have not, however, made any precise military convention earmarking particular troops as we do not think either of these contingencies probable. Dr. Salazar has now consented to the use of a "life-belt" by the British with Portuguese collaboration in the early part of October. As soon as we are established there and he is relieved from his anxieties, we shall press for extensions of these facilities to United States ships and aircraft.

The possession of the "life-belt" is of great importance to the sea war. The U-boats have quitted the North Atlantic, where convoys have been running without loss since the middle of May and have concentrated on the southern route. The use of the "life-belt" will be of the utmost help in attacks on them from the air. Besides this, there is the ferrying of United States heavy bombers to Europe and Africa, which is also most desirable. All the above is of most especially secret operational character.

A U G U S T 1 9 , 1 9 4 3

For Marshal Stalin
from President Roosevelt
and Prime Minister Churchill

Mr. Churchill and I are here, accompanied by our staffs, and will confer for a period of perhaps ten days. We are very desirous of emphasizing to you again the importance of our all three meeting. We at the same time entirely understand the strong reasons which cause you to be near the fronts of battle, fronts where your personal presence has been so fruitful of victory.

Neither Astrakhan nor Archangel are suitable, in our opinion. We are quite prepared, however, to go with appropriate officers to Fairbanks, Alaska. There, we may survey the entire picture, in common with you.

We are now at a crucial point in the war, a time presenting a unique chance for a rendezvous. Both Mr. Churchill and I earnestly hope you will give this opportunity your consideration once more.

If we are unable to agree on this very essential meeting between our three governmental heads, Churchill and I agree with you that we should in the near future arrange a meeting of foreign-office-level representatives. Final decisions must, of course, be left to our respective Governments, so such a meeting would be of an exploratory character.

In 38 days General Eisenhower and General Alexander have accomplished the conquest of Sicily.

The Axis defenders amounted to a total of 405,000 men: 315,000 Italians and 90,000 Germans. We attacked with 13 American and British divisions, suffering approximately 18,000 casualties (killed and wounded). The Axis forces lost

30,000 dead and wounded: 23,000 Germans and 7,000 Italians, collected and counted. There were 130,000 prisoners.

Italian forces on Sicily have been wiped out, with the exception of some few who took to the countryside in plain-clothes. There is a tremendous amount of booty, guns and planes, and munitions of all sorts lying about everywhere, including more than 1,000 airplanes captured on the various air fields.

As you have been informed previously, we will soon make a powerful attack on the mainland of Italy.

> ROOSEVELT
> CHURCHILL

AUGUST 19, 1943

Personal and Secret Message from Premier J. V. Stalin to the Prime Minister, Mr. W. Churchill, and the President, Mr. F. D. Roosevelt

Your joint message of August 19 has reached me.

I fully share your opinion and that of Mr. Roosevelt concerning the importance of a meeting between the three of us. At the same time, I earnestly request you to appreciate my position at a moment when our armies are exerting themselves to the utmost against the main forces of Hitler and when

Hitler, far from having withdrawn a single division from our front, has already moved, and keeps moving, fresh divisions to the Soviet-German front. At a moment like this, I cannot, in the opinion of all my colleagues, leave the front without injury to our military operations to go to so distant a point as Fairbanks, even though, had the situation on our front been different, Fairbanks would doubtless have been a perfectly suitable place for our meeting, as I indeed thought before.

As to a meeting between representatives of our states, and perhaps representatives in charge of foreign affairs, I share your view of the advisability of such a meeting in the near future. However, the meeting should not be restricted to the narrow bounds of investigation, but should concern itself with practical preparation so that after the conference our Governments might take specific decisions and thus avoid delay in reaching decisions on urgent matters.

Hence I think I must revert to my proposal for fixing beforehand the range of problems to be discussed by the representatives of the three states and drafting the proposals they will have to discuss and submit to our Governments for final decision.

2. Yesterday we received from Mr. Kerr the addenda and corrections to the joint message in which you and Mr. Roosevelt informed me of the instructions sent to General Eisenhower in connection with the surrender terms worked out for Italy during the discussions with General Castellano. I and my colleagues believe that the instructions given to General Eisenhower follow entirely from the thesis on Italy's unconditional surrender and hence cannot give rise to any objections.

Still, I consider the information received so far insufficient for judging the steps that the Allies should take in the negotiations with Italy. This circumstance confirms the necessity of Soviet participation in reaching a decision in the course of the negotiations. I consider it timely, therefore, to set up the military-political commission representing the three countries, of which I wrote to you on August 22.

AUGUST 24, 1943

Received on August 26, 1943

F. Roosevelt and W. Churchill
to J. V. Stalin

The following is the decision as to the military operations to be carried out during 1943 and 1944 which we have arrived at in our conference at Quebec just concluded. We shall continue the bomber offensive against Germany from bases in the United Kingdom and Italy on a rapidly increasing scale. The objectives of this air attack will be to destroy the air combat strength of Germany, to dislocate her military, economic and industrial system, and to prepare the way for an invasion across the Channel. A large-scale building-up of American forces in the United Kingdom is now under way. It will provide an assemblage force of American and British divisions for operations across the Channel. Once a bridgehead on the Continent has been secured, it will be reinforced steadily by additional American troops at the rate of from three to five divisions a month. This operation will be the primary American and British air and ground effort against the Axis. The war in the Mediterranean is to be pressed vigorously. In that area our objectives will be the elimination of Italy from the Axis alliance and the occupation of Italy, as well as of Corsica and Sardinia, as bases for operations against Germany. In the Balkans, operations will be limited to the supply by air and sea transport of the Balkan guerrillas, minor commando raids, and the bombarding of strategic objectives. In the Pacific and in Southeast Asia, we shall accelerate our operations against Japan. Our purposes are to exhaust the air, naval, and shipping resources of Japan, to cut her communications, and to secure bases from which Japan proper may be bombed.

Received on September 4, 1943

Secret and Personal Message from the President and the Prime Minister to Marshal Stalin

General Charlie has stated that the Italians accept and he is coming to sign, but we do not know for certain whether this statement refers to the short military terms, which have been seen by you, or to the more complete and comprehensive terms which your readiness to sign has been specifically indicated.

The military situation there is both critical and hopeful. The mainland invasion begins almost immediately while the heavy blow called "Avalanche" will be delivered in the next week or so. The difficulties of the Italian Government and people in escaping from the clutches of Hitler may make a still more daring move necessary, and for this General Eisenhower will require as much Italian help as he can get. The acceptance of the terms by the Italians is largely supported by the fact that we shall send an airborne division to Rome to help them hold off the Germans who have gathered Panzer strength near there and who may replace the Badoglio Government with a Quisling administration probably headed by Farinacci. We think, since matters are moving so fast there, that General Eisenhower should have discretion not to delay settlement with the Italians because of differences between the long and the short terms. The short terms, it is clear, are included in the long terms that they are based on unconditional surrender, and that clause ten of the short terms places the interpretation in the hands of the Allied Commander-in-Chief.

We are assuming, therefore, that you expect General Eisenhower to sign the short terms in your behalf, if that be necessary, to avoid the further journeying of General Charlie to Rome and the consequent delay and uncertainty affecting military operations.

We are, of course, anxious that the Italian unconditional surrender be to the Soviet Union as well as to the United States and Britain. The date of the surrender announcement must, of course, be fitted in with the military coup.

CHURCHILL
ROOSEVELT

Personal and Secret Message from Premier J. V. Stalin to the President, Mr. Franklin D. Roosevelt, and the Prime Minister, Mr. Winston Churchill

I have received your message of September 4. The question which you ask me—namely, whether the Soviet Government would agree to General Eisenhower signing on its behalf the short armistice terms for Italy—should be considered as having been answered in the letter which V. M. Molotov, People's Commissar for Foreign Affairs, wrote to Mr. Kerr, the British Ambassador, on September 2. The letter said that the powers which the Soviet Government entrusted to General Eisenhower also extended to his signing the short armistice terms.

S E P T E M B E R 7 , 1 9 4 3

Received on September 6, 1943

Personal and Secret Message from the President to Marshal Stalin

Both the Prime Minister and myself are pleased with the idea of a political and military meeting on the State Department level.

It should be held, I think, as soon as possible. Perhaps September 25 would be a good date. What do you think of this?

The Prime Minister has suggested London or some other place in England, and I should agree to have my representative go to either of these if you also think it best. I am inclined, however, to the thought of a more remote spot where the meeting would be less surrounded by reporters. Perhaps Casablanca or Tunis, and I do not object to Sicily, except that the communications from and to there are more troublesome.

The political representatives would, of course, report to their respective Governments, as I do not think we could give plenary powers to them. They could be advised on military developments by attaching one or two military advisers to them, although I do not want to have the meeting develop at this stage into a full-scale combined chiefs' conference.

If Mr. Molotov and Mr. Eden attend, I should wish to send Mr. Hull, but I do not want Mr. Hull to undertake such a long journey, so I would, therefore, send Mr. Welles, the Under Secretary of State. Mr. Harriman would also attend, as he has an excellent knowledge of shipping and commercial matters. I shall endeavor to send someone from my staff as American military adviser. He would be in complete touch with the work of the Combined Staffs.

May I congratulate you again on the tenacity and drive of your armies. It is magnificent.

While this coming conference is a very good thing, I still have the hope that you and Mr. Churchill and myself can meet as soon as possible. I, personally, could arrange to meet in a place as far as North Africa between November 15 and December 15. You will understand, I know, that I cannot be away for more than 20 days from Washington as, under our constitution, no one can sign for me while I am absent.

Why not send an officer to General Eisenhower's headquarters in connection with the commission to sit in Sicily on further settlements with the Italians? He would join the British and Americans who are now working on this very subject.

There is no objection, as far as I am concerned, to adding a French member to this commission, as we are now in the midst of equipping ten or eleven of their divisions in North Africa. It would, however, be very unwise to let the French take part in the discussions relating to the military occupation of Italy. If the Italians go through with the terms of surrender, which they have already signed, I hope they will wholeheartedly support the occupation troops. On the whole, the Italians dislike the French greatly, and if we bring the French into occupation discussions, the civil and military elements in Italy will resent it extremely.

The problem of consulting the Greeks and Yugoslavs can be discussed later on.

ROOSEVELT

Personal and Secret Message from Premier J. V. Stalin to the President, Mr. F. D. Roosevelt

I received on September 6 your message dealing with a number of important subjects.

I still think that the most pressing problem is to set up a three-Power military-political commission, with headquarters in Sicily, or in Algiers, to begin with. The dispatch of a Soviet officer to Gen. Eisenhower's headquarters can in no way replace the military-political commission, which is required to direct on-the-spot negotiations with Italy and with the Governments of other countries falling away from Germany. Much time has passed without things making the slightest headway.

As to French participation in the commission, I have already stated my opinion. However, if you have any doubts we can naturally discuss the matter after the three-Power commission is set up.

2. The time suggested by the Prime Minister for the meeting of our three representatives—early October—would be suitable; as to the place, I suggest Moscow. By that time the three Governments could agree on the range of subjects to be discussed, as well as on proposals relating to those problems; otherwise the conference will not yield the results which our Governments want.

3. As regards a personal meeting between us with Mr. Churchill participating, I, too, desire this as early as possible. The date suggested by you is acceptable to me. It would be advisable to select a country where all the three countries are represented, such as Iran. I should add, however, that we shall yet have to specify the date of meeting with due regard to the

situation on the Soviet-German front, where more than 500 divisions are engaged on both sides and where supervision by the Supreme Command of the U.S.S.R. is required almost daily.

4. Thank you for your congratulations on the successes of the Soviet armies. I take the occasion to congratulate you and the Anglo-American forces on their latest brilliant successes in Italy.

S E P T E M B E R 8 , 1 9 4 3

Received on September 10, 1943

F. Roosevelt and W. Churchill to J. V. Stalin

We are pleased to tell you that General Eisenhower has accepted the unconditional surrender of Italy, terms of which were approved by the United States, the Soviet Republics, and the United Kingdom.

Allied troops have landed near Naples and are now in contact with German forces. Allied troops are also making good progress in the southern end of the Italian peninsula.

Personal and Secret Message from Premier J. V. Stalin to the President, Mr. Roosevelt, and the Prime Minister, Mr. Churchill

I have received your message of September 10. I congratulate you on your latest success, particularly the landing in the Naples area. There can be no doubt that the landing in the Naples area and Italy's break with Germany will be yet another blow to Hitler Germany and considerably facilitate the Soviet armies' operations on the Soviet-German front.

So far the offensive of the Soviet troops is making good progress. I think we shall have further success in the next two or three weeks. It may be that we shall take Novorossiisk in a day or two.

SEPTEMBER 10, 1943

Received on September 11, 1943

Personal and Secret to Marshal Stalin from President Roosevelt

I thank you for your message received today.

I agree on the immediate setting up of the military-political commission, but think that Algiers would be better than Sicily if only because of communications and, therefore, suggest they meet in Algiers on Tuesday, 21 September. Full information will be given, of course, in regard to the progress of current and future negotiations, but they should not have plenary powers. Such authority would, of course, have to be referred to their governments before final action.

I am entirely willing to have a French representative on this commission. It is important to all of us that the secrecy of all their deliberations be fully maintained.

Regarding the meeting of our three representatives, I will cheerfully agree that the place of meeting be Moscow and the date the beginning of October—say Monday, the fourth. I will send you in two or three days a suggested informal list of subjects to be discussed, but I think the three members should feel free, after becoming acquainted with each other, to discuss any other matters which may come up.

I am delighted with your willingness to go along with the third suggestion, and the time about the end of November is all right. I fully understand that military events might alter the situation for you or for Mr. Churchill or myself. Meanwhile, we can go ahead on that basis. Personally, my only hesitation is the place, but only because it is a bit further away from Washington than I had counted on. My Congress will be in session at that time and, under our constitution, I must act on legislation within ten days. In other words, I must receive documents and return them to the Congress within ten days, and Tehran makes this rather a grave risk if the flying weather is bad. If the Azores route is not available, it means coming by way of Brazil and across the South Atlantic Ocean. For these reasons, I hope that you will consider some part of Egypt, which is also a neutral state, and where every arrangement can be made for our convenience.

I really feel that the three of us are making real headway.

Personal and Secret Message from Premier J. V. Stalin to the President, Mr. F. D. Roosevelt, and the Prime Minister, Mr. W. Churchill

I have received your messages of September 10.

Basically, the point about the military-political commission can be regarded as settled. We have appointed as the Soviet Ambassador A. Y. Vyshinsky, Deputy Chairman of the Council of People's Commissars and Deputy People's Commissar for Foreign Affairs, whom you know. A. Y. Bogomolov, the Soviet Ambassador to the Allied Governments in London, has been appointed his deputy. In addition, we are sending a group of responsible military and political experts and a small technical staff.

I think that the date September 25-30 should be fixed for the military-political commission getting down to work. I have nothing against the commission functioning in Algiers for a start and later deciding whether it should move to Sicily or elsewhere in Italy.

The Prime Minister's considerations regarding the functions of the commission are correct, in my view, but I think that later, taking into account the initial experience of the commission, we shall be able to specify its functions in respect of both Italy and other countries.

2. Concerning the meeting of our three representatives, I suggest that we consider it agreed that Moscow be the place, and the date, October 4, as suggested by the President.

As stated in previous messages, I still believe that for the conference to be a success, it is essential to know in advance the proposals that the British and U.S. Governments intend to submit to it. I do not, however, suggest any restrictions as far as the agenda is concerned.

3. As regards the meeting of the three heads of the Governments, I have no objection to Tehran, which, I think, is a more suitable place than Egypt, where the Soviet Union is not yet represented.

SEPTEMBER 12, 1943

Personal and Most Secret Message from the Prime Minister, Mr. Winston Churchill, to Marshal J. V. Stalin

Now that Mussolini has been set up by the Germans as head of a so-called Republican Fascist Government, it is essential to counter this movement by doing all we can to strengthen the authority of the King and Badoglio, who signed the armistice with us and have since faithfully carried it out to the best of their ability, and surrendered the bulk of their fleet. Besides, for military reasons, we must mobilize and concentrate all the forces in Italy which are anxious to fight or at least obstruct the Germans. These are already active.

I propose therefore to advise the King to appeal on the wireless to the Italian people to rally round the Badoglio Government and to announce his intention to build up a broad-based anti-fascist coalition government, it being understood that nothing shall be done to prevent the Italian people from settling what form of democratic government they will have after the war.

It should also be said that useful service by the Italian Government's army and people against the enemy will be recognized in the adjustment and working of the armistice; but that while the Italian Government is free to declare war on Germany, this will not make Italy an ally, but only a co-belligerent.

I want at the same time to insist on the signing of the comprehensive armistice terms which are still outstanding, even though some of those terms cannot be enforced at the present time. Against this Badoglio would be told that the Allied Governments intend to hand over the historic mainland of Italy, Sicily, and Sardinia to the administration of the Italian Government under the Allied Control Commission as it is freed from the enemy.

I am putting these proposals also to President Roosevelt, and I hope I may count on your approval. As you will readily understand, the matter is vitally urgent for military reasons. For instance, the Italians have already driven the Germans out of Sardinia, and there are many islands and key points which they still hold and which we may get.

S E P T E M B E R   2 1 ,   1 9 4 3

Personal and Secret to Marshal Stalin from President Roosevelt

Your wire has reached me and our delegation will be in Moscow on October 15th. While I do not consider this conference as one to plan or recommend military strategy, I have no objection to and would welcome the widest exchange of views of your proposal relating to an expedition directed against France.

General Deane, who is to be a member of our mission, will be informed fully of our plans and intentions.

That this is a three-Power conference and that any discussion on our proposal should be limited to the future intentions and plans of these three Powers exclusively is agreeable to me. This would, of course, in no way preclude a wider participation at some later date and under circumstances which would be mutually acceptable to our three Governments.

I am sure that we are going to find a meeting of minds for the important decisions which must finally be made by us. And so this preliminary conference will explore the ground, and if difficulties develop at the meeting of our Foreign Ministers, I would still have every hope that they can be reconciled when you and Mr. Churchill and I meet.

It appears that the American and British armies should enter Rome in another few weeks.

OCTOBER 4, 1943

Personal and Secret
from Premier J. V. Stalin
to President Franklin D. Roosevelt

Your message of October 4 received.

Regarding military matters, that is, Anglo-American measures to shorten the war, you already know the Soviet Government's point of view from my previous message. It is still my hope that in this respect a preliminary three-Power conference will be useful and clear the ground for further important decisions.

If I have understood you aright, the Moscow conference will confine itself to discussing matters bearing on our three countries only; hence we can take it as agreed that a four-Power declaration is not to be on the agenda.

Our representatives should do their best to overcome the difficulties that may arise in their responsible work. As to decisions, they can, of course, only be taken by our Governments—I hope when you, Mr. Churchill, and myself meet in person.

I wish the U.S. and British armies successful fulfilment of their mission and entry into Rome, which will be another blow to Mussolini and Hitler.

OCTOBER 14, 1943

Received on October 25, 1943

Personal and Secret for Marshal Stalin

Your message in regard to our meeting was received today (October 21). I am deeply disappointed.

Your reason for needing daily guidance from and your personal contact with the Supreme Command, which is causing such outstanding results, is fully appreciated by me. Please accept my assurance on that.

All this is of high importance, and I wish you would realize that there are other vital matters which, in our constitutional American Government, are my fixed obligations. These I cannot change. Under our constitution, legislation must be acted on by the President within ten days after such legislation has been passed. In other words, the President must receive and return to Congress physical documents, with his written approval or veto, within this period. As I have told you previously, I cannot do this by cable or radio.

The difficulty with Tehran is this simple fact. The over-the-mountain approach to that city often makes flying impossible for some days at a time. This risk of delay is double, both for the plane delivering documents from Washington and for the one returning these documents to Congress. I regret to say that, as the head of the nation, it is impossible for me to go to a place where it is impossible to fulfill my obligations under our constitution.

The flying risks for documents up to and including the low country as far as the Gulf of Persia can be assumed by me through a relay system of planes. I cannot assume, however, the delays suffered by flights over the mountains in both directions into the saucer where Tehran lies. With much regret, therefore, I must tell you that I cannot go to Tehran. My cabinet members and legislative leaders are in complete agreement on this.

One last practical suggestion, however, can be made. Let all three of us go to Basra, where we shall be perfectly protected in three camps, established and guarded by our respective troops. You can have easily, as you know, a special telephone, controlled by you, laid from Basra to Tehran where it would connect with your own line into Russia. All your needs should be met by such a wire service, and by plane you will only be a little further off from Russia than at Tehran itself.

I do not consider in any way the fact that from United States territory I would have to travel to within six hundred miles from Russian territory.

I must carry on a constitutional government more than one hundred and fifty years old. Were it not for this fact, I would gladly go ten times the distance to meet you.

Your obligation to your people to carry on the defeat of our common enemy is great, but I am begging you not to forget my great obligation to the American Government and toward maintenance of the all-out United States war effort.

I look upon our three meeting as of the greatest possible importance; this not only as regards our people of today, but also in the light of a peaceful world for generations to come. This I have told you before.

Future generations would look upon it as a tragedy if a few hundred miles caused yourself, Mr. Churchill, and me to fail.

I say again that I would go to Tehran gladly if limitations over which I have no control did not prevent me.

Because of your communications problem, may I suggest Basra.

If this does not appeal to you, may I hope deeply you will think again of Bagdad or Asmara, or even Ankara. I think the latter place is worth considering. It is in neutral territory. The Turks might think well of the idea of being hosts. Of course, this has not been mentioned by me to them or to anyone else.

Please do not fail me in this crisis.

ROOSEVELT

Personal and Secret to Marshal Stalin from President Roosevelt

The problem of my going to the place you suggested is becoming so acute that I feel that I should tell you frankly that, for constitutional reasons, I cannot take the risk. The Congress will be in session. New laws and resolutions must be acted on by me after their receipt and must be returned to the Congress physically before ten days have elapsed. None of this can be done by radio or cable. The place you mentioned is too far to be sure that the requirements are fulfilled. The possibility of delay in getting over the mountain—first east-bound and then west-bound—is insurmountable. We know from experience that planes in either direction are often held up for three or four days.

I do not think that any one of us will need legation facilities as each of us can have adequate personal and technical staffs. I venture, therefore, to make some other suggestions and I hope you will consider them or suggest any other place where I can be assured of meeting my constitutional obligations.

In many ways Cairo is attractive, and I understand there is a hotel and some villas out near the pyramids which could be completely segregated. Asmara, the former Italian capital of Eritrea, is said to have excellent buildings and a landing field —good at all times.

Then there is the possibility of meeting at some port in the Eastern Mediterranean, each one of us to have a ship. If this idea attracts you, we could easily place a fine ship entirely at your disposal for you and your party so that you would be completely independent and, at the same time, be in constant contact with your own war front.

Another suggestion is in the neighborhood of Bagdad, where we could have three comfortable camps with adequate Russian, British, and American guards. This last idea seems worth considering.

In any event, I think the press should be entirely banished, and the whole place surrounded by a cordon so that we would not be disturbed in any way. What would you think of November 20th or November 25th as the date of the meeting?

I am placing a very great importance on the personal and intimate conversations which you and Churchill and I will have for on them depend the hopes of the future world.

Your continuous initiative along your whole front heartens all of us.

OCTOBER 14, 1943

Personal and Secret
to President Franklin D. Roosevelt
from Premier J. V. Stalin

With regard to the place for the meeting of the three heads of the Governments, I should like to inform you of the following.

I am afraid I cannot accept as suitable any one of the places suggested by you as against Tehran. It is not a matter of security, for that does not worry me.

In the course of the Soviet troops' operations in the summer and autumn of this year, it became evident that our forces would be able to continue their offensive operations against the German Army and that the summer campaign would thus continue into winter. My colleagues hold that the operations necessitate day-to-day guidance by the Supreme Command and my personal contact with the Command. In Tehran, unlike the other places, these requirements can be met by communicating directly with Moscow by telegraph or telephone. For this reason my colleagues insist on Tehran.

I agree that the press should be barred. I also accept your proposal for fixing November 20 or 25 as possible dates for the meeting.

Mr. Hull has arrived safely in Moscow, and I hope his attendance at the Moscow three-Power conference will be very useful.

OCTOBER 19, 1943

Message to President Roosevelt from Marshal Stalin and Prime Minister Churchill

In an informal discussion, we have taken a preliminary view of the situation as it affects us and have planned out the course of our meetings, social and others. We have invited Messrs. Mikolajczyk, Romer, and Grabski to come at once for further conversations with us and with the Polish National Committee. We have agreed not to refer in our discussions to the Dumbarton Oaks issues, and that these shall be taken up when we three can meet together. We have to consider the best way of reaching an agreed policy about the Balkan countries, including Hungary and Turkey. We have arranged for Mr. Harriman to sit in as an observer at all the meetings, where business of importance is to be transacted, and for General Deane to be present whenever military topics are raised. We have arranged for technical contacts between our high officers and General Deane on military aspects, and for any meetings which may be necessary later in our presence and that which I have already mentioned to Mr. Hull. I could be fully replaced at that meeting by my First Deputy in the Government, V. M. Molotov, who, during the discussions, will enjoy, in keeping with our Constitution, the rights of head of the Soviet Government. In that case, the difficulties of choosing a place would disappear. I hope this suggestion will at the moment be found suitable.

N O V E M B E R   5 ,   1 9 4 3

Received on November 24, 1943

Personal and Secret for Marshal Stalin from President Roosevelt

This morning I arrived in Cairo and have begun discussions with the Prime Minister. By the end of the week, conference will follow with the Generalissimo, after which he will return to China. Then the Prime Minister and myself, accompanied by our senior staffs, can proceed to Tehran to meet you, Mr.

Molotov, and your staff officers. I could arrive the afternoon of November 29, if it meets with your convenience. I am prepared to remain for two to four days, depending upon how long you can stay away from your compelling responsibilities. If you would telegraph me what day you wish to set for the meeting and how long you could stay, I would be very grateful. I would appreciate your keeping me informed of your plans as I realize bad weather often causes delays in travel from Moscow to Tehran at this time of the year.

I understand that your Embassy and the British Embassy in Tehran are placed close together, whereas my Legation is some distance away. I am informed that all three of us would be incurring unnecessary risks while driving to and from our meetings if we were staying too far apart.

Where do you think we should live?

It is with keen anticipation that I look forward to our conversations.

Personal and Secret for Marshal Stalin from President Roosevelt

The destination of our party has been reached in safety, and all of us earnestly hope that by this time you also have arrived safely. I consider the conference to have been a great success, and it was an historic event, I feel sure, in the assurance not only of our ability to wage war together, but also to work for the peace to come in utmost harmony. Our personal talks together were enjoyed very much by me, and particularly the opportunity of meeting with you face to face. I look forward to seeing you again sometime, and, until that time, I wish the greatest success to you and your armies.

DECEMBER 4, 1943

Received on December 7, 1943

Secret and Personal from President Roosevelt to Marshal Stalin

It has been decided to appoint General Eisenhower immediately to the command of cross-Channel operations.

Received on December 7, 1943

Secret and Personal from the President and Prime Minister to Marshal Stalin

In the Conference just concluded in Cairo, we have reached the following decisions regarding the conduct of the war against Germany in 1944 in addition to the agreements arrived at by the three of us at Tehran.

With the purpose of dislocating the German military, economic and industrial system, destroying the German air combat strength, and paving the way for an operation across the Channel the highest strategic priority will be given to the bomber offensive against Germany.

The operation scheduled for March in the Bay of Bengal has been reduced in scale in order to permit the reinforcement of amphibious craft for the operation against Southern France.

We have directed the greatest effort be made to increase the production of landing craft in the United States and Great Britain to provide reinforcement of cross-Channel operations. The diversion from the Pacific of certain landing craft has been ordered for the same purpose.

Secret and Personal
to President Roosevelt
from Premier Stalin

I have received your message about the appointment of General Eisenhower. I welcome it. I wish him success in preparing and carrying out the forthcoming decisive operations.

DECEMBER 10, 1943

Received on February 25, 1944

Personal and Secret
to President Roosevelt
from Premier Stalin

Thank you for your telegram.

I agree that the Tehran Conference was a great success and that our personal meetings were of great importance in many respects. I hope the common enemy of our peoples—Hitler Germany—will soon feel this. Now there is certainty that our peoples will cooperate harmoniously, both at present and after the war.

I wish you and your armed forces the best of success in the coming momentous operations.

I also hope that our meeting in Tehran will not be the last and that we shall meet again.

DECEMBER 6, 1943

PART IV

1944

Received on January 23, 1944

Message from Mr. Churchill
and President Roosevelt
to Marshal Stalin
(Secret and Personal)

With regard to the handing over to Soviet Russia of the Italian shipping asked for by the Soviet Government at the Moscow Conference and agreed to with you by us both at Tehran, we have received a memorandum by the Combined Chiefs of Staff contained in our immediately following telegram. For the reasons set out in this memorandum, we think it would be dangerous to our triple interests actually to carry out any transfer or to say anything about it to the Italians until their cooperation is no longer of operational importance.

Nevertheless, if after full consideration you desire us to proceed, we will make a secret approach to Marshal Badoglio with a view to concluding the necessary arrangements without their becoming generally known to the Italian naval forces. If, in this way, agreement could be reached, such arrangements with the Italian naval authorities as were necessary could be left to him. These arrangements would have to be on the lines that the Italian ships selected should be sailed to suitable Allied ports where they would be collected by Russian crews, who would sail into Russian northern ports which are the only ones open where any refitting necessary would be undertaken.

We are, however, very conscious of the dangers of the above course for the reasons we have laid before you, and we have therefore decided to propose the following alternative, which from the military point of view has many advantages.

The British battleship *Royal Sovereign* has recently completed refitting in the United States. She is fitted with radar for all types of armament. The United States will make one light cruiser available at approximately the same time.

His Majesty's Government and the United States Government are willing, for their part, that these vessels should be taken over at British ports by Soviet crews and sailed to North Russian ports. You could then make such alterations as you find necessary for Arctic conditions.

These vessels would be temporarily transferred on loan to Soviet Russia and would fly the Soviet flag until, without prejudice to military operations, the Italian vessels can be made available.

His Majesty's Government and the United States Government will each arrange to provide 20,000 tons of merchant shipping to be available as soon as practicable and until the Italian merchant ships can be obtained without prejudice to the projected essential operations "Overlord" and "Anvil."

This alternative has the advantage that the Soviet Government would obtain the use of the vessels at a very much earlier date than if they all had to be refitted and rendered suitable for northern waters. Thus, if our efforts should take a favorable turn with the Turks, and the Straits become open, these vessels would be ready to operate in the Black Sea. We hope you will very carefully consider this alternative, which we think is in every way superior to the first proposal.

> *CHURCHILL*
> *ROOSEVELT*

Received on January 23, 1944

Message from
Mr. Churchill and President Roosevelt
to Marshal Stalin
(Most Secret and Personal)

Our immediately preceding telegram.

Our Combined Chiefs of Staff have made the following positive recommendation with supporting data:

(a) The present time is inopportune for effecting the transfer of captured Italian ships because of pending Allied operations.

(b) To impose the transfer at this time would remove needed Italian resources now employed in current operations and would interfere with their assistance now being given by Italian repair facilities. It might cause scuttling of Italian warships and result in the loss of Italian cooperation, thus jeopardizing "Overlord" and "Anvil."

(c) At the earliest moment permitted by operations, the implementation of the delivery of the Italian vessels may proceed.

CHURCHILL
ROOSEVELT

Received on February 1, 1944

Message from Mr. Churchill
to Marshal Stalin
(Most Secret and Personal)

On Thursday last, accompanied by the Foreign Secretary and with the authority of the War Cabinet, I saw representatives of the Polish Government in London. I informed them that the security of the Russian frontiers against Germany was a matter of high consequence to His Majesty's Government and that we should certainly support the Soviet Union in all measures we considered necessary to that end. I remarked that Russia had sustained two frightful invasions with immense slaughter and devastation at the hands of Germany, that Poland had had her national independence and existence restored after the First World War, and that it was the policy of the great Allies to restore Poland once again after this war. I said that although we had gone to war for the sake of Poland, we had not gone for any particular frontier line, but for the existence of a strong, free, independent Poland which Marshal Stalin declared himself as supporting. Moreover, although Great Britain would have fought on in any case for years until something happened to Germany, the liberation of Poland from Germany's grip is being achieved mainly by the enormous sacrifices of the Russian armies. Therefore, the Allies had a right to ask that Poland should be guided to a large extent about the frontiers of the territory she would have.

2. I then said that I believed from what had passed at Tehran that the Soviet Government would be willing to agree

to the easterly frontiers of Poland conforming to the Curzon Line subject to the discussion of ethnographical considerations, and I advised them to accept the Curzon Line as a basis for discussion. I spoke of the compensations which Poland would receive in the North and in the West. In the North there would be East Prussia; but here I did not mention the point about Königsberg. In the West they would be secure and aided to occupy Germany up to the line of the Oder. I told them it was their duty to accept this task and guard their frontiers against German aggression towards the East in consequence of their liberation by the Allied forces. I said in this task they would need a friendly Russia behind them and would, I presume, be sustained by the guarantee of the three Great Powers against further German attack. Great Britain would be willing to give such a guarantee if it were in harmony with her ally, Soviet Russia. I could not forecast the action of the United States but it seemed that the three Great Powers would stand together against all disturbers of the peace, at any rate until a long time after the war was ended. I made it clear that the Polish Government would not be committed to agree to the Curzon Line as a basis of examination except as part of the arrangement which gave them the fine compensations to the North and to the West which I had mentioned.

3. Finally, I said that if the Russians' policy was unfolded in the sense I had described, I would urge the Polish Government to settle on that basis and His Majesty's Government would advocate the confirmation of such a settlement by the Peace Conference or by the conferences for the settlement of Europe following the destruction of Hitlerism, and would support no territorial claims from Poland which went beyond it. If the Polish Ministers were satisfied that agreement could be reached upon these lines, it would be their duty at the proper time not merely to acquiesce in it, but to commend it to their people with courage, even though they ran the risk of being repudiated by extremists.

4. The Polish Ministers were very far from rejecting the prospects thus unfolded, but they asked for time to consider the matter with the rest of their colleagues, and as a result of this they have asked a number of questions none of which seem to be in conflict with the general outline of my suggestions to them. In particular, they wish to be assured that Po-

land would be free and independent in the new home assigned
to her; that she would receive the guarantee of the Great
Powers against German revenge effectively; that these Great
Powers would also assist in expelling the Germans from the
new territories to be assigned to Poland; and that in the regions to be incorporated in Soviet Russia such Poles as wished
would be assisted to depart for their new abodes. They also
inquired about what their position will be if a large part of
Poland west of the Curzon Line is to be occupied by the advancing Soviet armies. Will they be allowed to go back and
form a more broad-based government in accordance with the
popular wish and allowed to function administratively in the
liberated areas in the same way as other governments which
have been overrun? In particular they are deeply concerned
about the relations between the Polish underground movement
and the advancing Soviet forces, it being understood that their
prime desire was to assist in driving out the Germans. This
underground movement raises matters important to our common war effort.

5. We also attach great importance to assimilating our action in the different regions which we hope to liberate. You
know the policy we are following in Italy. There we have
taken you fully into our councils, and we want to do the same
in regard to France and the other countries to whose liberation
we look forward. We believe such uniformity of action is of
great importance now and in the future to the cause of the
United Nations.

6. The earliest possible agreement in principle on the frontiers of the new Polish State is highly desirable to allow a
satisfactory arrangement regarding these two very important
points.

7. While, however, everyone will agree that Soviet Russia
has the right to recognize or refuse recognition to any foreign
government, do you not agree that to advocate changes within
a foreign government comes near to that interference in internal sovereignty to which you and I have expressed ourselves
opposed? I may mention that this view is strongly held by His
Majesty's Government.

8. I now report this conversation, which expresses the policy of His Majesty's Government at the present time upon this
difficult question, to my friend and comrade Marshal Stalin. I

earnestly hope these plans may be helpful. I had always hoped to postpone discussions of frontier questions until the end of the war, when the victors would be round the table together. The dangers which have forced His Majesty's Government to depart from this principle are formidable and imminent. If, as we may justly hope, the successful advance of the Soviet armies continues and a large part of Poland is cleared of German oppressors, a good relationship will be absolutely necessary between whatever forces can speak for Poland and the Soviet Union. The creation in Warsaw of another Polish Government different from the one we have recognized up to the present, together with disturbances in Poland, would raise an issue in Great Britain and the United States detrimental to that close accord between the three Great Powers upon which the future of the world depends.

9. I wish to make it clear that this message is not intended to be any intervention or interference between the Governments of the Soviet Union and Poland. It is a statement in broad outline of the position of His Majesty's Government in Great Britain in regard to a matter in which they feel themselves deeply concerned.

10. I should like myself to know from you what steps you would be prepared to take to help us all to resolve this serious problem. You could certainly count on our good offices for what they would be worth.

11. I am sending a copy of this message to the President of the United States with a request for complete secrecy.

Personal and Secret
from Premier J. V. Stalin
to the Prime Minister,
Mr. Winston Churchill

Your message on the Polish question has reached me through Mr. Kerr, who arrived in Moscow a few days ago and with whom I had a useful talk.

I see you are giving a good deal of attention to the problem of Soviet-Polish relations. All of us greatly appreciate your efforts.

I have the feeling that the very first question which must be completely cleared up even now is that of the Soviet-Polish frontier. You are right, of course, in noting that on this point Poland should be guided by the Allies. As for the Soviet Government, it has already stated, openly and clearly, its views on the frontier question. We have stated that we do not consider the 1939 boundary final, and have agreed to the Curzon Line, thereby making very important concessions to the Poles. Yet the Polish Government has evaded our proposal for the Curzon Line, and in its official statements continues to maintain that the frontier imposed upon us under the Riga Treaty is final. I infer from your letter that the Polish Government is prepared to recognize the Curzon Line, but, as is known, the Poles have not made such a statement anywhere.

I think the Polish Government should officially state in a declaration that the boundary line established by the Riga Treaty shall be revised and that the Curzon Line is the new boundary line between the U.S.S.R. and Poland. It should state that as officially as the Soviet Government has done by declaring that the 1939 boundary line shall be revised and that the Soviet-Polish frontier should follow the Curzon Line.

As regards your statement to the Poles that Poland could considerably extend her frontiers in the West and North, we are in agreement with that with, as you are aware, one amendment. I mentioned the amendment to you and the President in Tehran. We claim the transfer of the northeastern part of East Prussia, including the port of Königsberg as an ice-free one, to the Soviet Union. It is the only German territory claimed by us. Unless this minimum claim of the Soviet Union is met, the Soviet Union's concession in recognizing the Curzon Line becomes entirely pointless, as I told you in Tehran.

Lastly, about the composition of the Polish Government. I think you realize that we cannot re-establish relations with the present Polish Government. Indeed, what would be the use of re-establishing relations with it when we are not at all certain that tomorrow we shall not be compelled to sever those relations again on account of another fascist provocation on its part, such as the "Katyn affair"? Throughout the recent period the Polish Government, in which the tone is set by Sosnkowski, has not desisted from statements hostile to the Soviet Union. The extremely anti-Soviet statements of the Polish Ambassadors in Mexico and Canada and of Gen. Anders in the Middle East, the hostility displayed towards the Soviet Union by Polish underground publications in German-occupied territory, a hostility which transcends all bounds, the annihilation, on directions from the Polish Government, of Polish guerrillas fighting the Hitler invaders, these and many other pro-fascist actions of the Polish Government are known. That being so, no good can be expected unless the composition of the Polish Government is thoroughly improved. On the other hand, the removal from it of profascist imperialist elements and the inclusion of democratic-minded people would, one is entitled to hope, create the proper conditions for normal Soviet-Polish relations, for solving the problem of the Soviet-Polish frontier and, in general, for the rebirth of Poland as a strong, free, and independent state. Those interested in improving the composition of the Polish Government along these lines are primarily the Poles themselves, the broad sections of the Polish people. By the way, last May you wrote to me saying that the composition of the

Polish Government could be improved and that you would
work towards that end. You did not at that time think that this
would be interference in Poland's internal sovereignty.

With reference to the questions posed by the Polish Ministers and mentioned in paragraph 4 of your letter, I think there
will be no difficulty in reaching agreement on them.

FEBRUARY 4, 1944

Personal and Secret Message
from Premier J. V. Stalin
to the President, Mr. F. D. Roosevelt,
and the Prime Minister,
Mr. W. Churchill

I have received your message on the negotiations with the
Italians and on the new armistice terms for Italy. Thank you
for the information.

Mr. Eden advised Sobolev that Moscow had been kept
fully informed of the negotiations with Italy. I must say, however, that Mr. Eden's statement is at variance with the facts,
for I received your message with large omissions and without
the closing paragraphs. It should be said, therefore, that the
Soviet Government has not been kept informed of the Anglo-
American negotiations with the Italians. Mr. Kerr assures me
that he will shortly receive the full text of your message, but
three days have passed and Ambassador Kerr has yet to give it
to me. I cannot understand how this delay could have come

about in transmitting information on so important a matter.

2. I think the time is ripe for us to set up a military-political commission of representatives of the three countries—the U.S.A., Great Britain, and the U.S.S.R.—for consideration of problems related to negotiations with various Governments falling away from Germany. To date it has been like this: the U.S.A. and Britain reach agreement between themselves while the U.S.S.R. is informed of the agreement between the two Powers as a third party looking passively on. I must say that this situation cannot be tolerated any longer. I propose setting up the commission and making Sicily its seat for the time being.

3. I am looking forward to receiving the full text of your message on the negotiations with Italy.

A U G U S T 2 2 , 1 9 4 3

————————

Received on February 27, 1944

Most Secret and Personal Message from Mr. Winston Churchill to Marshal Stalin

The Secretary of State for Foreign Affairs and I have had numerous long discussions with the Polish Prime Minister and the Minister for Foreign Affairs. I shall not attempt to repeat all the arguments which were used, but only to give what I conceive to be the position of the Polish Government in the upshot.

The Polish Government are ready to declare that the Riga Line no longer corresponds to realities and, with our participation, to discuss with the Soviet Government, as part of the general settlement, a new frontier between Poland and the Soviet Union, together with the future frontiers of Poland in the North and West. Since, however, the compensations which Poland is to receive in the North and West cannot be stated publicly or precisely at the present time, the Polish Government clearly cannot make an immediate public declaration of their willingness to cede territory as indicated above because the publication of such an arrangement would have an entirely one-sided appearance, with the consequence that they would immediately be repudiated by a large part of their people abroad and by the underground movement in Poland with which they are in constant contact. It is evident therefore that the Polish-Soviet territorial settlement, which must be an integral part of the general territorial settlement of Europe, could only formally be agreed and ratified when the victorious Powers are gathered round the table at the time of an armistice or peace.

For the above reasons the Polish Government, until it had returned to Polish territory and been allowed to consult the Polish people, can obviously not formally abdicate its rights in any part of Poland as hitherto constituted, but vigorous prosecution of the war against Germany in collaboration with the Soviet armies would be greatly assisted if the Soviet Government will facilitate the return of the Polish Government to liberated territory at the earliest possible moment; and in consultation with their British and American Allies as the Russian armies advance, arrange from time to time with the Polish Government for the establishment of the civil administration of the Polish Government in given districts. The procedure would be in general accordance with those to be followed in the case of other countries as they are liberated. The Polish Government are naturally very anxious that the districts to be placed under Polish civil administration should include such places as Vilna and Lvov, where there are concentrations of Poles, and that the territories to the east of the demarcation line should be administered by Soviet military authorities with the assistance of representatives of the United Nations. They point out that thus they would be in the best position to enlist all such able-bodied Poles in the war effort. I have informed them and they clearly understand that you will not assent to leaving Vilna and Lvov under Polish administration. I wish, on the other hand, to be able to assure them that the area to be placed under Polish civil administration will include at least all Poland west of the Curzon Line.

At the frontier negotiations contemplated in paragraph 2 above, the Polish Government, taking into consideration the mixed character of the population of Eastern Poland, would favor a frontier drawn with a view to assuring the highest degree of homogeneity on both sides, while reducing as much as possible the extent and hardship of an exchange of populations. I have no doubt myself, especially in view of the immediate practical arrangements contemplated by the Polish Government set out in paragraph 3 above, that these negotiations will inevitably lead to the conclusion you desire in regard to the future of the Polish-Soviet frontier, but it seems to me unnecessary and undesirable publicly to emphasize this at this stage.

As regards the war with Germany, which they wish to prosecute with the utmost vigor, the Polish Government realize that it is imperative to have a working agreement with the Soviet Government in view of the advance of the liberating armies on to Polish soil, from which these armies are driving the German invader. They assure me emphatically that they have at no time given instructions to the underground movement to attack "partisans." On the contrary, after consultation with the leaders of their underground movement and with these people, they have issued orders for all Poles now in arms or about to revolt against Hitlerite tyranny as follows:

When the Russian army enters any particular district in Poland, the underground movement is to disclose its identity and meet the requirements of the Soviet commanders, even in the absence of a resumption of Polish-Soviet relations. The local Polish military commander, accompanied by the local civilian underground authority, will meet and declare to the commander of incoming Soviet troops that, following the instructions of the Polish Government, to which they remain faithful, they are ready to co-ordinate their actions with him in the fight against the common foe.

These orders, which are already in operation, seem to me,

as I am sure they will to you, of the highest significance and importance.

For the first time, on February 6th, I told the Polish Government that the Soviet Government wished to have the frontier in East Prussia drawn to include, on the Russian side, Königsberg. The information came as a shock to the Polish Government, who see in such a decision substantial reduction in the size and in the economic importance of the German territory to be incorporated in Poland by way of compensation. But I stated that, in the opinion of His Majesty's Government, this was a rightful claim on the part of Russia. Regarding, as I do, this war against German aggression as all one and as a thirty-years' war from 1914 onwards, I reminded M. Mikolajczyk of the fact that the soil of this part of East Prussia was dyed with Russian blood expended freely in the common cause. Here the Russian armies advancing in August 1914 and winning the battle of Gumbinnen and other actions had, with their forward thrusts and with much injury to their mobilization, forced the Germans to recall two army corps from the advance on Paris which withdrawal was an essential part in the victory of the Marne. The disaster at Tannenberg did not in any way undo this great result. Therefore it seemed to me that the Russians had a historic and well-founded claim to this German territory.

As regards the composition of the Polish Government, the Polish Government cannot admit any right of a foreign intervention. They can, however, assure the Russian Government that by the time they have entered into diplomatic relations with the Soviet Government, they will include among themselves none but persons fully determined to cooperate with the Soviet Union. I am of the opinion that it is much better that such changes should come about naturally and as a result of further Polish consideration of their interests as a whole. It might well be in my opinion that the moment for a resumption of these relations in a formal manner would await the reconstitution of a Polish Government at the time of the liberation of Warsaw, when it would arise naturally from the circumstances attending that glorious event.

It would be in accordance with the assurances I have received from you that in an agreement covering the points made above, the Soviet Government should join with His

Majesty's Government in undertaking vis-à-vis each other and Poland, first to recognize and respect the sovereignty, independence, and territorial integrity of reconstituted Poland and the right of each to conduct its domestic affairs without interference, and secondly to do their best to secure in due course the incorporation in Poland of the Free City of Danzig, Oppeln, Silesia, East Prussia, west and south of a line running from Königsberg, and of as much territory up to the Oder as the Polish Government see fit to accept; thirdly, to effect the removal from Poland including the German territories to be incorporated in Poland of the German population; and fourthly, to negotiate the procedure for the exchange of population between Poland and the Soviet Union and for the return to the Mother Country of the nationals of the Powers in question. All the undertakings to each other on the part of Poland, the Soviet Union, and the United Kingdom should, in my view, be drawn up in such a form that they could be embodied in a single instrument or exchange of letters.

I informed the Polish Ministers that should the settlement which has now been outlined in the various telegrams that have passed between us become a fact and be observed in spirit by all the parties to it, His Majesty's Government would support that settlement at the Conference after the defeat of Hitler and also that we would guarantee that settlement in after years to the best of our ability.

LONDON, FEBRUARY 20th, 1944

From Premier J. V. Stalin to the Prime Minister, Mr. W. Churchill (Secret and Personal)

Both messages of February 20 on the Polish question reached me through Mr. Kerr on February 27.

Now that I have read the detailed record of your conversations with the leaders of the Polish émigré Government, I am more convinced than ever that men of their type are incapable of establishing normal relations with the U.S.S.R. Suffice it to point out that they, far from being ready to recognize the Curzon Line, claim both Lvov and Vilna. As regards the desire to place certain Soviet territories under foreign control, we cannot agree to discuss such encroachments, for, as we see it, the mere posing of the question is an affront to the Soviet Union.

I have already written to the President that the time is not yet ripe for a solution of the problem of Soviet-Polish relations. I am compelled to reaffirm the soundness of this conclusion.

MARCH 3, 1944

Message from Mr. Churchill
to Marshal Stalin
(Most Secret and Personal)

I thank you for your message of March 3rd about the Polish question.

2. I made it clear to the Poles that they would not get either Lvov or Vilna, and references to these places, as my message shows, merely suggested a way in those areas in which Poles thought they could help the common cause. They were certainly not intended to be insulting either by the Poles or by me. However, since you find them an obstacle, pray consider them withdrawn and expunged from the message.

3. Proposals I submitted to you make the occupation by Russia of the Curzon Line a *de facto* reality in the agreement with the Poles from the moment your armies reach it, and I have told you that provided the settlement you and we have outlined in our talks and correspondence was brought into being, His Britannic Majesty's Government would support it at the armistice or peace conferences. I have no doubt that it would be equally supported by the United States. Therefore you would have the Curzon Line *de facto* with the assent of the Poles as soon as you get there, and with the blessing of your Western Allies at the general settlement.

4. Force can achieve much, but force supported by the good will of the world can achieve more. I earnestly hope that you will not close the door finally to a working arrangement with the Poles which will help the common cause during the war and give you all you require at the peace. If nothing can be arranged and you are unable to have any relations with the Polish Government which we shall continue to recognize as

the government of the ally for whom we declared war upon Hitler, I should be very sorry indeed. The War Cabinet ask me to say that they would share this regret. Our only comfort will be that we have tried our very best.

5. You spoke to Ambassador Clark Kerr of the danger of the Polish question making a rift between you and me. I shall try earnestly to prevent this. All my hopes for the future of the world are based upon the friendship and cooperation of the Western democracies and Soviet Russia.

LONDON, MARCH 7, 1944

Secret and Personal for Marshal Stalin from President Roosevelt

A number of important steps have been taken in recent months by the Governments of the United Nations toward laying the foundations for post-war cooperative action in the various fields of international economic relations. You will recall that the United Nations Conference on Food and Agriculture, held in May 1943, gave rise to an interim commission which is now drafting recommendations to lay before the various Governments for a permanent organization in this field. More recently, the United Nations Relief and Rehabilitation Administration has been established and is now in operation.

There have been for nearly a year informal technical discussions at the expert level among many of the United Nations on mechanisms for international monetary stabilization; these discussions are preparatory to a possible convocation of a

United Nations monetary conference. Similar discussions have been taking place, though on a more restricted scale, with regard to the possibility of establishing mechanisms for facilitating international development investment. Also, to some extent, informal discussions have taken place among some of the United Nations with regard to such questions as commercial policy, commodity policy, and cartels. Discussions are in contemplation on such questions as commercial aviation, oil, and others. A conference of the International Labor Organization will take place in April, in part for the purpose of considering its future activities.

The need for both informal discussions and formal conferences on various economic problems was emphasized in a document presented by the Secretary of State at the Moscow meeting of Foreign Ministers entitled "Bases of Our Program for International Economic Cooperation." It was suggested that "the time has come for the establishment of a commission comprising representatives of the principal United Nations and possibly certain others of the United Nations for the joint planning of the procedures to be followed in these matters." It is clear to me that there is a manifest need for United Nations machinery for joint planning of the procedures by which consideration should be given to the various fields of international economic cooperation, the subjects which should be discussed, the order of discussion, and the means by which existing and prospective arrangements and activities are to be coordinated.

It is not my purpose at this time and in this connection to raise the broader issues of international organization for the maintenance of peace and security. Preliminary discussions on this subject are currently in contemplation between our three Governments under the terms of the Moscow Protocol. What I am raising here is the question of further steps toward the establishment of United Nations machinery for post-war economic collaboration, which was raised at the Moscow meeting by the Secretary of State and was discussed at Tehran by you, Prime Minister Churchill, and myself.

I should very much appreciate it if you would give me your views on the suggestion made by the Secretary of State at Moscow, together with any other thoughts as to the best procedure to be followed in this extremely important matter.

Secret and Personal
from Premier J. V. Stalin
to the President, Mr. Roosevelt

Your message on post-war economic cooperation to hand. The problems of international economic cooperation, raised in Mr. Hull's Memorandum, are undoubtedly of great importance and merit attention. I think it quite timely to set up a United Nations staff to study them and to specify ways and means of examining the various aspects of international economic cooperation in keeping with the decisions of the Moscow and Tehran conferences.

MARCH 10, 1944

Received on March 23, 1944

For Marshal Stalin
from President Roosevelt

Ambassador Harriman has just informed me that the Soviet Union is not planning to participate in the conference of the International Labor Organization starting April 2 in Philadelphia.

I have given considerable thought to the role that the International Labor Organization should play in constantly improving the labor and social standards throughout the world. I am anxious that you should know about this matter.

The International Labor Organization should be, in my opinion, the instrument for the formulation of international policy on matters directly affecting the welfare of labor and for international collaboration in this field. I should like to see it become a body which will serve as an important organ of the United Nations for discussing economic and social matters relating to labor and an important agency for consideration of international economic policies which look directly toward improvement in standards of living. It would be unfortunate if both our Governments did not take advantage of the conference in Philadelphia to help develop our common objectives. We could thereby adapt the existing International Labor Organization to the tasks facing the world without loss of time.

The United States Government delegates to the Philadelphia Conference are being instructed by me to propose measures to broaden the activities and functions of the International Labor Organization and raise the question of its future relationship to other international organizations. In view of your interest in these matters and since there is a great range of social and economic problems that are of common interest to both our Governments, I greatly hope that your Government will participate in this conference.

Personal and Secret
from Premier J. V. Stalin
to the President, Mr. F. Roosevelt

I share your desire for cooperation between our two Governments in studying economic and social problems linked with improving the welfare of labor on an international scale. The Soviet Union cannot, however, send representatives to the International Labor Organization conference in Philadelphia for the reasons set forth in the letter to Mr Harriman, because the Soviet trade unions are opposed to participation in it, and the Soviet Government cannot but take account of the opinion of the trade unions.

It goes without saying that if the International Labor Organization were to become an agency of the United Nations, not of the League of Nations, with which the Soviet Union cannot associate itself, Soviet participation would be possible. I hope that this will become feasible and the appropriate steps taken in the near future.

MARCH 25, 1944

Message from Mr. Churchill and President Roosevelt to Marshal Stalin (Personal and Most Secret)

Pursuant to our talks at Tehran, the general crossing of the sea will take place around "R" date, which Generals Deane and Burrows have recently been directed to give to the Soviet General Staff. We shall be acting at our fullest strength.

2. We are launching an offensive on the Italian mainland at maximum strength about mid-May.

3. Since Tehran, your armies have been gaining a magnificent series of victories for the common cause. Even in the month when you thought they would not be active, they have gained these great victories. We send you our very best wishes and trust that your armies and ours, operating in unison in accordance with our Tehran agreement, will crush the Hitlerites.

ROOSEVELT
CHURCHILL

APRIL 18th, 1944

Secret and Personal
from Premier J. V. Stalin
to the President, Mr. F. Roosevelt,
and the Prime Minister,
Mr. W. Churchill

Your message of April 18 received.

The Soviet Government is gratified to learn that in accordance with the Tehran agreement the sea crossing will take place at the appointed time, which Generals Deane and Burrows have already imparted to our General Staff, and that you will be acting at full strength. I am confident that the planned operation will be a success.

I hope that the operations you are undertaking in Italy will likewise be successful.

As agreed in Tehran, the Red Army will launch a new offensive at the same time so as to give maximum support to the Anglo-American operations.

Please accept my thanks for the good wishes you have expressed on the occasion of the Red Army's success. I subscribe to your statement that your armies and our own, supporting each other, will defeat the Hitlerites and thus fulfil their historic mission.

APRIL 22, 1944

Received on May 14, 1944

Joint Message
from President Roosevelt
and Prime Minister Churchill
to Marshal Stalin

In order to give the maximum strength to the attack across the sea against Northern France, we have transferred part of our landing craft from the Mediterranean to England. This, together with the need for using our Mediterranean land forces in the present Italian battle, makes it impracticable to attack the Mediterranean coast of France simultaneously with the "Overlord" assault. We are planning to make such an attack later, for which purpose additional landing craft are being sent to the Mediterranean from the United States. In order to keep the greatest number of German forces away from Northern France and the Eastern Front, we are attacking the Germans in Italy at once on a maximum scale and, at the same time, are maintaining a threat against the Mediterranean coast of France.

ROOSEVELT
CHURCHILL

Secret and Personal
from Premier J. V. Stalin
to the President, Mr. F. Roosevelt,
and the Prime Minister,
Mr. W. Churchill

Your joint message received. You can best decide how and in what way to allocate your forces. The important thing, of course, is to ensure complete success for "Overlord." I express confidence also in the success of the offensive launched in Italy.

MAY 15, 1944

Secret and Personal
from President Roosevelt
to Marshal Stalin

I would appreciate receiving your views on my making a statement to be issued after "D" day along the following lines in place of a tripartite statement to be issued by the Soviet, United States, and British Governments:

"A suggestion has been made that the Allied Governments issue a joint statement to the people of Germany and their sympathizers in which emphasis would be placed on the recent landings made on the European continent. I have not agreed with this as it might overemphasize the importance of these landings. What I desire to impress upon the German people and their sympathizers is that their defeat is inevitable. I also wish to emphasize to them that it is unintelligent, on their part, to continue in the war from now on. They must realize in their hearts that, with their present objectives and their present leaders, it is inevitable that they will be totally defeated.

"From now on, every German life that is lost is an unnecessary loss. It is true, from a cold-blooded point of view, that the Allies will also suffer losses. However, the Allies outnumber so greatly Germany in population and in resources that the Germans on a relative basis will be much harder hit—down to the last family—than the Allies, and mere stubbornness will never help Germany in the long run. It has been made abundantly clear by the Allies that they do not seek the total destruction of the people of Germany. What they seek is the total destruction of the philosophy of those Germans who have stated that they could subjugate the world.

"The Allies desire to attain the long-range goal of human freedom—greater real liberty—political, intellectual, and religious, and a greater justice, economic and social.

"We are being taught by our times that no group of men can ever be sufficiently strong to dominate the entire world. The United States Government and the people of the United States—with almost twice the population of Germany—send word to the German people that this is the time for them to abandon the teachings of evil.

"By far the greater part of the population of the world of nearly two billion people feel the same way. It is only Germany and Japan who stand out against all the rest of humanity.

"In his heart every German knows that this is true. Germany and Japan have made a disastrous and terrible mistake. Germany and Japan must atone reasonably for the wanton destruction of lives and property which they have committed. They must renounce the philosophy which has been imposed upon them—the falsity of this philosophy must be very clear to them now.

"The more quickly the fighting and the slaughter shall terminate, the more rapidly shall arrive a more decent civilization in the entire world.

"The attacks which the American, the British, and the Soviet armies and their associates are now making in the European theater will, we hope, continue with success. However, the people of Germany must realize that these attacks are only a part of many which will increase in volume and number until victory, which is inevitable, is attained."

Prime Minister Churchill has agreed to follow me with a message along the above lines.

M A Y   2 3 ,   1 9 4 4

His Excellency Joseph V. Stalin, Supreme Commander of the Armed Forces, the Union of Soviet Socialist Republics

Moscow

My dear Marshal Stalin,

I am sending to you two scrolls for Stalingrad and Leningrad which cities have won the wholehearted admiration of the American people. The heroism of the citizens of these two cities and the soldiers who so ably defended them has not only been an inspiration to the people of the United States, but has served to bind even more closely the friendship of our two nations. Stalingrad and Leningrad have become synonyms for the fortitude and endurance which has enabled us to resist and

will finally enable us to overcome the aggression of our enemies.

I hope that in presenting these scrolls to the two cities you
will see fit to convey to their citizens my own personal ex-
pressions of friendship and admiration and my hope that our
people will continue to develop that close understanding
which has marked our common effort.

Very sincerely yours,
Franklin D. ROOSEVELT

MAY 25, 1944

Secret and Personal
from Premier J. V. Stalin
to the President, Mr. F. Roosevelt

Your communication on a statement to the people of Germany has reached me.

In view of the experience of the war against the Germans
and the German character I do not think that your suggested
statement would have a positive effect, seeing that it is to be
synchronized with the beginning of the landing and not with
the moment when the Anglo-American landing and the forthcoming offensive of the Soviet armies will have registered
notable success.

As to the nature of the statement, we can return to this
when circumstances favor publication.

MAY 26, 1944

From Premier J. V. Stalin
to the President
of the U.S.A., Mr. Roosevelt

I congratulate you on the taking of Rome—a grand victory for the Allied Anglo-American troops.
The news has caused deep satisfaction in the Soviet Union.

JUNE 5, 1944

Sent on June 7, 1944

Secret and Personal to the President,
Mr. F. Roosevelt,
from Premier J. V. Stalin

I feel it necessary to let you know that on June 6, in reply to a message from Mr. Churchill I sent the following personal message about the plan for a Soviet summer offensive.

"Your communication on the successful launching of 'Overlord' has reached me. It is a source of joy to us all and of hope for further successes.

"The summer offensive of the Soviet troops, to be

launched in keeping with the agreement reached at the Tehran Conference, will begin in mid-June in one of the vital sectors of the front. The general offensive will develop by stages, through consecutive engagement of the armies in offensive operations. Between late June and the end of July, operations will turn into a general offensive of the Soviet troops.

"I shall not fail to keep you posted about the course of the operations.

" J U N E 6 , 1 9 4 4 "

Personal and Most Secret Message from Mr. Churchill to Marshal Stalin

Everything has started well. The mines, obstacles and land batteries have been largely overcome. The air landings were very successful and on a large scale. Infantry landings are proceeding rapidly, and many tanks and self-propelled guns are already ashore.

The weather outlook is moderate to good.

J U N E 6 , 1 9 4 4

Secret and Personal
from Premier J. V. Stalin to the Prime
Minister, Mr. W. Churchill

Your communication on the successful launching of "Overlord" has reached me. It is a source of joy to us all and of hope for further successes.

The summer offensive of the Soviet troops, to be launched in keeping with the agreement reached at the Tehran Conference, will begin in mid-June in one of the vital sectors of the front. The general offensive will develop by stages, through consecutive engagement of the armies in offensive operations. Between late June and the end of July, the operations will turn into a general offensive of the Soviet troops.

I shall not fail to keep you posted about the course of the operations.

J U N E 6 , 1 9 4 4

Received on June 19, 1944

Personal and Secret for Marshal Stalin from President Roosevelt

Mr. Mikolajczyk, the Polish Prime Minister, has, as you know, just completed a brief visit to Washington and for reasons which Ambassador Harriman has already explained to you I considered his visit to be desirable and necessary at this time.

Therefore you are aware that his visit was not connected with any attempt on my part to inject myself into the merits of the differences which exist between the Polish Government in Exile and the Soviet Government. Although we had a frank and beneficial exchange of views on a wide variety of subjects affecting Poland, I can assure you that no specific plan or proposal in any way affecting Polish-Soviet relations was drawn up. I believe, however, that you would be interested in my personal impression of Mr. Mikolajczyk and of his attitude toward the problems with which his country is confronted.

Mr. Mikolajczyk impressed me as a very sincere and reasonable man whose sole desire is to do what is best for his country. He is fully cognizant that the whole future of Poland depends upon the establishment of genuinely good relations with the Soviet Union and to achieve that end will, in my opinion, make every effort.

The vital necessity for the establishment of the fullest kind of collaboration between the Red Army and the forces of the Polish underground in the common struggle against our enemy is his primary immediate concern. He believes that coordination between your armies and the organized Polish under-

ground is a military factor of the highest importance not only
to your armies in the East but also to the main task of finishing
off the Nazi beast in his lair by our combined efforts.

It is my impression that the Prime Minister is thinking only
of Poland and the Polish people and will not allow any petty
considerations to stand in the way of his efforts to reach a
solution with you. In fact it is my belief that he would not
hesitate to go to Moscow, if he felt that you would welcome
such a step on his part, in order to discuss with you personally
and frankly the problems affecting your two countries, particularly the urgency of immediate military collaboration. I know
you will understand that in making this observation I am in no
way attempting to press upon you my personal views in a
matter which is of special concern to you and your country. I
felt, however, that you were entitled to have a frank account
of the impressions I received in talking with Premier Mikolajczyk.

Secret and Personal
to the President, Mr. F. Roosevelt
from Premier J. V. Stalin

I am in a position to inform you that not later than a week
from now the Soviet armies will start the second round of their
offensive. It will involve 130 divisions, including armoured
ones. I and my colleagues anticipate important success. I hope
that it will be a substantial help to the Allied operations in
France and Italy.

J U N E   2 1 ,   1 9 4 4

Secret and Personal
to the President, Mr. F. Roosevelt, from Premier J. V. Stalin

Thank you for informing me of your meeting with Mr. Mikolajczyk.

If we have in view military cooperation between the Red Army and the Polish underground forces fighting the Hitler invaders, that, undoubtedly, is vital to the final defeat of our common enemy. Certainly, the proper solution of the problem of Soviet-Polish relations is of great importance in this respect. You are aware of the Soviet Government's point of view and of its desire to see Poland strong, independent and democratic, and Soviet-Polish relations good-neighbourly and based on lasting friendship. A vital condition for this, in the view of the Soviet Government, is a reconstruction of the Polish émigré Government that would ensure participation of Polish leaders in Britain, the U.S.A. and the U.S.S.R., and more particularly of Polish democratic leaders inside Poland, plus recognition by the Polish Government of the Curzon Line as the new frontier between the U.S.S.R. and Poland.

I must say, however, that Mr. Mikolajczyk's Washington statement makes it appear that he has not made a step forward on this point. Hence at the moment I find it hard to express an opinion about a visit to Moscow by Mr. Mikolajczyk.

We all greatly appreciate your attention to Soviet-Polish relations and your efforts in this field.

M O S C O W , J U N E 2 4 , 1 9 4 4

————————

Secret and Personal
from Premier J. V. Stalin
to the Prime Minister,
Mr. W. Churchill

Your message of June 25 received.

Meanwhile the Allied troops have liberated Cherbourg, thus crowning their efforts in Normandy with another major victory. I welcome the continuing success of the gallant British and U.S. troops who are developing their operations both in Northern France and in Italy.

While the scale of the operations in Northern France is becoming more and more powerful and menacing for Hitler, the successful development of the Allied offensive in Italy, too, is worthy of the greatest attention and praise. We wish you further success.

With regard to our offensive, I may say that we shall give the Germans no respite, but shall go on extending the front of our offensive operations, increasing the force of our drive against the German armies. You will agree, I suppose, that this is essential for our common cause.

As to Hitler's flying bomb, this weapon, as we see, cannot seriously affect either the operations in Normandy or the population of London, whose courage is a matter of record.

JUNE 27, 1944

Secret and Personal to the President, Mr. F. Roosevelt, from Premier J. V. Stalin

Your message about the two scrolls for Stalingrad and Leningrad has reached me. They were handed to me by Ambassador Harriman and will be forwarded to their destinations. Upon receiving the scrolls I made the following statement:

"I accept President Roosevelt's scrolls as a symbol of the fruitful cooperation between our two countries in the name of the freedom of our nations and of human progress.

"The scrolls will be handed to the representatives of Leningrad and Stalingrad."

2. Please accept my heartfelt gratitude for your high commendation of the efforts exerted by Stalingrad and Leningrad in the struggle against the German invaders.

JUNE 27, 1944

Personal and Most Secret Message from Mr. Churchill to Marshal Stalin

Your message of June 27th has given us all the greatest encouragement and pleasure. I am forwarding it to the President, who will, I am sure, be gratified.

2. This is the moment for me to tell you how immensely we are all here impressed with the magnificent advances of the Russian armies which seem, as they grow in momentum, to be pulverizing the German armies which stand between you and Warsaw, and afterwards Berlin. Every victory that you gain is watched with eager attention here. I realize vividly that all this is the second round you have fought since Tehran, the first which regained Sebastopol, Odessa, and the Crimea and carried your vanguards to the Carpathians, Sereth, and Prut.

3. The battle is hot in Normandy. The June weather has been very tiresome. Not only did we have a gale on the beaches worse than any in the summer-time records for many years, but there has been a great deal of cloud. This denies us full use of our overwhelming air superiority and also helps flying bombs to get through to London. However, I hope July will show an improvement. Meanwhile, the hard fighting goes in our favor, and, although eight Panzer divisions are in action against the British sector, we still have a good majority of tanks. We have well over three-quarters of a million British and Americans ashore, half and half. The enemy is burning and bleeding on every front at once, and I agree with you that this must go on to the end.

J U L Y   1 ,   1 9 4 4

To Marshal Joseph V. Stalin

Moscow

My dear Marshal,

Just as I was leaving on this trip to the Pacific, I received the very delightful framed photograph of you which I consider excellent. I am particularly happy to have it and very grateful to you.

The speed of the advance of your armies is amazing, and I wish much that I could visit you to see how you are able to maintain your communications and supplies to the advancing troops.

We have taken the key island of Saipan after rather heavy losses, and are at this moment engaged in the occupation of Guam. At the same time, we have just received news of the difficulties in Germany and especially at Hitler's headquarters. It is all to the good. With my very warm regards, I am

Very sincerely yours,
Franklin D. ROOSEVELT

JULY 21, 1944

Secret and Personal
from Premier J. V. Stalin
to the President, Mr. F. Roosevelt

I share your opinion about the desirability of a meeting between you, Mr. Churchill, and myself.

I must say, however, that now, with the Soviet armies deeply involved in fighting along so vast a front, it is impossible for me to leave the country and withdraw myself for any length of time from direction of front affairs. My colleagues consider it absolutely impossible.

J U L Y   2 2 ,   1 9 4 4

Secret and Personal
from Premier J. V. Stalin
to the Prime Minister,
Mr. W. Churchill

In connection with your latest message, I have given proper instructions on the experimental station in Debice. General Slavin, a General Staff representative, will establish the necessary contact on this matter with Generals Burrows and Deane. I appreciate the British Government's great interest in this matter. I promise, therefore, to take personal care of the matter so as to do all that can be done according to your wishes.

I was deeply satisfied to learn from you that your troops in Normandy have broken into the German rear. I wish you further success.

J U L Y   2 2 ,   1 9 4 4

Secret and Personal
from Premier J. V. Stalin
to the Prime Minister,
Mr. W. Churchill

Your message of July 20 received. I am now writing to you on the Polish question only.

Events on our front are going forward at a very rapid pace. Lublin, one of Poland's major towns, was taken today by our troops, who continue their advance.

In this situation, we find ourselves confronted with the practical problem of administration on Polish territory. We do not want to, nor shall we, set up our own administration on Polish soil, for we do not wish to interfere in Poland's internal affairs. That is for the Poles themselves to do. We have, therefore, seen fit to get in touch with the Polish Committee of National Liberation, recently set up by the National Council of Poland, which

Received on July 28, 1944

Personal and Secret for Marshal Stalin from President Roosevelt

In view of the rapid military progress now being made, I can fully understand the difficulty of your coming to a conference with the Prime Minister and me, but I hope you can keep very much in mind such a conference and that we can meet as early as possible. We are approaching the time for further strategical decisions, and such a meeting would help me domestically.

Secret and Personal from Premier Stalin to the President, Mr. F. Roosevelt

I have received your messages of July 28.
I share your opinion concerning the importance of a meeting, but circumstances connected with the operations on our

front, of which I apprised you last time, prevent me, unfortunately, from reckoning on the possibility of a meeting in the immediate future.

As regards the Polish question, the matter hinges primarily on the Poles themselves and on the ability of members of the Polish émigré Government to cooperate with the Committee of National Liberation which is already functioning in Poland and to which the democratic forces of Poland are rallying more and more. For my part I am ready to render all Poles whatever assistance I can.

AUGUST 2, 1944

Secret and Personal
from Premier J. V. Stalin
to the President, Mr. F. D. Roosevelt

I should like to inform you of my meeting with Mikolajczyk, Grabski and Romer. My talk with Mikolajczyk convinced me that he has inadequate information about the situation in Poland. At the same time I had the impression that Mikolajczyk is not against ways being found to unite the Poles.

As I do not think it proper to impose any decision on the Poles, I suggested to Mikolajczyk that he and his colleagues should meet and discuss their problems with representatives of the Polish Committee of National Liberation, first and foremost the matter of early unification of all democratic forces on liberated Polish soil. Meetings have already taken place. I have been informed of them by both parties. The National Committee delegation suggested the 1921 Constitution as a basis for the Polish Government and expressed readiness if the Mikolajczyk group acceded to the proposal, to give it four portfolios, including that of Prime Minister for Mikolajczyk. Mikolajczyk, however, could not see his way to accept. I regret to say the meetings have not yet yielded the desired results. Still, they were useful because they provided Mikolajczyk and Morawski as well as Beirut, who had just arrived from Warsaw, with the opportunity for an exchange of views and particularly for informing each other that both the Polish National Committee and Mikolajczyk are anxious to cooperate and to seek practical opportunities in that direction. That can be considered as the first stage in the relations between the Polish Committee and Mikolajczyk and his colleagues. Let us hope that things will improve.

I understand the Polish Committee of National Liberation in Lublin has decided to invite Professor Lange to join it and take charge of foreign affairs. If Lange, a well-known Polish democratic leader, were enabled to go to Poland in order to assume that office it would undoubtedly promote Polish unity and the struggle against our common enemy. I hope you share this view and will for your part not withhold your support in this matter, which is so very important to the Allied cause.

AUGUST 9, 1944

Received on August 12, 1944

Personal and Secret for Marshal Stalin from President Roosevelt

I have received your telegram of August 9 and am most grateful for the résumé you have been good enough to give me of Prime Minister Mikolajczyk's conversations with you and the Polish Committee in Moscow.

It is as you know my earnest hope that there will emerge from these conversations some solution satisfactory to all concerned and which will permit an interim legal and truly representative Polish Government to be formed.

I am sure you recognize the difficulty of this Government taking official action at this stage in regard to Lange. He as a private citizen has of course every right under law to do what he sees fit, including the renunciation of his American citizenship. I am sure you will understand why, under the circumstances and particularly pending the outcome of the conversations between Premier Mikolajczyk, whose government we still officially recognize, and the Polish Committee, the Government of the United States does not want to become involved in the request of the Polish Committee that Professor Lange join it as head of the section on Foreign Affairs, nor to express any opinion concerning this request.

Secret and Personal
from Premier J. V. Stalin
to the President, Mr. F. Roosevelt,
and the Prime Minister,
Mr. W. Churchill

The message from you and Mr. Churchill about Warsaw has reached me. I should like to state my views.

Sooner or later the truth about the handful of power-seeking criminals who launched the Warsaw adventure will out. Those elements, playing on the credulity of the inhabitants of Warsaw, exposed practically unarmed people to German guns, armour and aircraft. The result is a situation in which every day is used, not by the Poles for freeing Warsaw, but by the Hitlerites, who are cruelly exterminating the civilian population.

From the military point of view the situation, which keeps German attention riveted to Warsaw, is highly unfavourable both to the Red Army and to the Poles. Nevertheless, the Soviet troops, who of late have had to face renewed German counter-attacks, are doing all they can to repulse the Hitlerite sallies and go over to a new large-scale offensive near Warsaw. I can assure you that the Red Army will stint no effort to crush the Germans at Warsaw and liberate it for the Poles. That will be the best, really effective, help to the anti-Nazi Poles.

AUGUST 22, 1944

Secret and Personal
from Premier J. V. Stalin
to the President, Mr. F. Roosevelt

I have received your message about participation of the Soviet Union Republics in the International Security Organization.

I attach the utmost importance to the statment made by the Soviet Delegation on the subject. Since the constitutional changes in our country early this year, the Governments of the Union Republics have been taking very careful note of the friendly countries' reaction to the extension of their rights in international relations, set down in the Soviet Constitution. You know, of course, that the Ukraine and Byelorussia, for instance, which are members of the Soviet Union, surpass some countries in population and political importance, countries which we all agree should be among the founders of the International Organisation. I hope, therefore, to have an opportunity of explaining to you the political importance of the question raised by the Soviet Delegation at Dumbarton Oaks.

S E P T E M B E R 7 , 1 9 4 4

Received on September 9, 1944

Personal and Secret for Marshal Stalin from President Roosevelt

I have had an interesting and pleasant talk with your Ambassador on the progress of the talks at Dumbarton Oaks. One issue of importance only apparently remains on which we have not yet reached agreement. This is the question of voting in the Council. We and the British both feel strongly that in the decisions of the Council, parties to a dispute should not vote even if one of the parties is a permanent member of the Council, whereas I gather from your Ambassador that your Government holds a contrary view.

Traditionally, since the founding of the United States, parties to a dispute have never voted on their own case. I know that public opinion in the United States would never understand or support a plan of international organization which violated this principle. I know, furthermore, that many nations of the world hold this same view, and I am fully convinced that the smaller nations would find it difficult to accept an international organization in which the Great Powers insisted upon the right to vote in the Council in disputes involving themselves. They would most certainly see in this an attempt on the part of the Great Powers to set themselves up above the law. I would have real trouble with the Senate.

I hope, for these reasons, that you will find it possible to instruct your Delegation to agree to our suggestion on voting. The talks at Dumbarton Oaks can be speedily concluded with complete and outstanding success if this can be done.

I hope you will appreciate the importance of these considerations and that we shall arrive at an agreed decision on this
matter.

S E P T E M B E R   1 4 ,   1 9 4 4

Personal and Secret Message
to Marshal Stalin
from the United States Government
and His Majesty's Government

We have arrived at the following decisions as to military
operations in our conference at Quebec just concluded:

Northwest Europe—Our intention is to press on with all
speed to destroy the German armed forces and penetrate into
the heart of Germany. The best opportunity to defeat the
enemy in the West lies in striking at the Ruhr and the Saar,
since the enemy will concentrate there the remainder of his
available forces in the defense of these essential areas. The
northern line of approach clearly has advantages over the
southern, and it is essential that before bad weather sets in we
should open up the northern ports, particularly Rotterdam and
Antwerp. It is on the left, therefore, that our main effort will
be exerted.

2. Italy—Our present operations in Italy will result in either: (A) The forces of Kesselring will be routed, in which
event it should be possible to undertake a rapid regrouping and
a pursuit toward the Ljubljana Gap; or (B) Kesselring will

succeed in effecting an orderly retreat, in which event we may have to be content this year with the clearing of the plains of Lombardy.

The progress of the battle will determine our future action. Plans are being prepared for an amphibious operation to be carried out, if the situation so demands, on the Istrian Peninsula.

3. The Balkans—We will continue operations of our air forces and commando type operations.

4. Japan—With the ultimate objective of invading the Japanese homeland, we have agreed on further operations to intensify in all theaters the offensive against the Japanese.

5. Plans were agreed upon for the prompt transfer of power after the collapse of Germany to the Pacific theater.

> *ROOSEVELT*
> *CHURCHILL*

SEPTEMBER 19, 1944

Secret and Personal
from Premier J. V. Stalin
to the President, Mr. F. Roosevelt

I have received the message from you and Mr. Churchill about the Quebec Conference, informing me of your future military plans. Your communication shows the important tasks ahead of the U.S. and British armed forces. Allow me to wish you and your armies every success.

At present, Soviet troops are mopping up the Baltic group of German forces which threatens our right flank. Without wiping out this group, we shall not be able to thrust deep into Eastern Germany. Besides, our forces have two immediate aims: to knock Hungary out of the war and to probe the German defenses on the Eastern Front and, if the situation proves favorable, pierce them.

S E P T E M B E R   2 9 ,   1 9 4 4

Received on October 5, 1944

Personal and Secret for Marshal Stalin from President Roosevelt

Although it had been my hope that the next meeting could have been between you, Churchill, and myself, I appreciate that the Prime Minister wished to have a conference with you at an early date.

I am sure you understand that in this global war there is literally no question, military or political, in which the United States is not interested. I am firmly convinced that the three of us, and only the three of us, can find the solution of the questions still unresolved. In this sense, while appreciating Mr. Churchill's desire for the meeting, I prefer to regard your forthcoming talks with the Prime Minister as preliminary to a meeting of the three of us which can take place any time after the elections here, as far as I am concerned.

I am suggesting, under the circumstances, if you and the

Prime Minister approve, that my Ambassador in Moscow be present at your coming conference as an observer for me. Mr. Harriman naturally would not be in position to commit this Government in respect to the important matters which very naturally will be discussed by you and Mr. Churchill.

By this time you will have received from General Deane the statement of the position of our Combined Chiefs of Staff regarding the war against Japan, and I want to reiterate to you how completely I accept the assurances on this point that you have given us. Our three countries are waging a successful war against Germany, and surely we can join together with no less success in crushing a nation which is, I am sure, as great an enemy of Russia as of us.

Secret and Personal
from Premier J. V. Stalin
to the President, Mr. F. Roosevelt

I was somewhat puzzled by your message of October 5. I had imagined that Mr. Churchill was coming to Moscow in keeping with an agreement reached with you at Quebec. It appears, however, that my supposition is at variance with reality.

I do not know what points Mr. Churchill and Mr. Eden want to discuss in Moscow. Neither of them has said anything to me so far. In a message, Mr. Churchill expressed the wish to come to Moscow if it was all right with me. I agreed, of course. That is how matters stand with the Churchill visit to Moscow.

I shall keep you informed, according as I clear up things with Mr. Churchill.

OCTOBER 8, 1944

Secret and Personal
from Premier J. V. Stalin
to the President, Mr. F. Roosevelt

During the stay of Mr. Churchill and Mr. Eden in Moscow, we exchanged views on a number of issues of common interest. Ambassador Harriman will assuredly have informed you of all the important talks. I also know that the Prime Minister intended sending you his appraisal of the talks. For my part, I can say that they were very useful in acquainting us with each other's views on such matters as the future of Germany, the Polish question, policy on the Balkans, and major problems of future military policies. The talks made it plain that we can without undue difficulty coordinate our policies on all important issues and that even if we cannot ensure immediate solution of this or that problem, such as the Polish question, we have, nevertheless, more favorable prospects in this respect as well. I hope that the Moscow talks will be useful, also, in other respects, that when we three meet we shall be able to take specific decisions on all the pressing matters of common interest to us.

2. Ambassador Gromyko has informed me of his recent

talk with Mr. Hopkins, who told him that you could arrive at the Black Sea late in November and meet with me on the Soviet Black Sea coast. I should very much welcome your doing so. My talk with the Prime Minister convinced me that he shares the idea. In other words, the three of us could meet late in November to examine the questions that have piled up since Tehran. I shall be glad to hear from you about this.

O C T O B E R   1 9 ,   1 9 4 4

Received on October 21, 1944

For Marshal Stalin
from President Roosevelt
(Personal and Secret)

We have been giving active consideration to the diplomatic recognition of the existing French authorities as the Provisional Government of France. These authorities have been made more representative of the French people by the recent enlargement of the consultative assembly. It is expected that the French, with the agreement of General Eisenhower, will set up in the very near future a real zone of the interior which will be under French administration, and that when this is done, it would be an appropriate time to recognize French authorities as the Provisional Government of France. I am informing you of our intentions in this regard in advance in the event that you may wish, when the zone of the interior is set up under French administration, to take some similar action.

Secret and Personal
from Premier J. V. Stalin
to the President, Mr. F. Roosevelt

I have received your message of October 21 concerning your intention to recognize the existing French authorities as the Provisional Government of France and to establish a zone of the interior under French administration. The British Government, too, has notified the Soviet Government of its desire to recognize the Provisional Government of France. As regards the Soviet Union, it welcomes the decision to recognize the French Provisional Government and has already given proper instructions to its representative in Paris.

O C T O B E R   2 2 ,   1 9 4 4

Received on October 25, 1944

Top Secret and Personal
for Marshal Stalin
from President Roosevelt

I am delighted to learn from reports made by Ambassador Harriman and from your message of October 19 of the success attained by you and the Prime Minister in approaching agreement on a number of questions of high interest to all of us in our common desire to secure and maintain a durable and satisfactory peace. I am sure that the progress made during your conversations in Moscow will facilitate and expedite our work in the next meeting when we three should come to a full agreement on our future activities, policies, and mutual interests.

All of us must investigate the practicability of various places where our November meeting can be held, i.e., from the standpoint of living accommodations, security, accessibility, and so forth. I would appreciate receiving your suggestions.

I have been considering the practicability of Cyprus, Athens, or Malta, in the event that my entering the Black Sea on a ship should be too difficult or impracticable. I prefer traveling and living on a ship. We know that security and living conditions in Cyprus and Malta are satisfactory.

I am looking forward to seeing you again with much pleasure.

I would be pleased to have your advice and suggestions.

Secret and Personal
from Premier J. V. Stalin
to the President, Mr. F. Roosevelt

Your message of October 25 to hand.

If a meeting on the Soviet Black Sea coast, as suggested by you earlier, is all right with you, I should think it highly desirable to carry out that plan. Conditions are quite favorable for a meeting there. I hope the safe entry of your ship into the Black Sea will also be possible by that time. My doctors advise, for the time being, against long journeys, so I must take their view into account.

I shall be glad to see you if you find it possible to make the voyage.

O C T O B E R   2 9 ,   1 9 4 4

———————

Sent on November 9, 1944

For President Roosevelt

Washington

I congratulate you on your re-election. I am confident that under your tried and tested leadership the American people will, jointly with the peoples of the Soviet Union, Great Britain, and the other democratic countries, round off the struggle against the common foe and ensure victory in the name of liberating mankind from Nazi tyranny.

J. STALIN

———————

Received on November 11, 1944

Personal from the President
for Marshal Stalin

I am very pleased to have your message of congratulations and happy that you and I can continue together with our Allies to destroy the Nazi tyrants and establish a long period of peace in which all of our peoples, freed from the burdens of war, may reach a higher order of development and culture, each in accordance with its own desires.

———————

Received on November 19, 1944

Personal and Top Secret
for Marshal Stalin
from the President

We are all three of us of one mind that we should meet very soon, but problems, chiefly geographic, do not make this easy at this moment. Under difficulties, I can arrange to go somewhere now in order to get back here by Christmas, but frankly it would be far more convenient if I could postpone it until after my inauguration on the 20th of January.

My naval authorities strongly recommend against the Black Sea. They do not want to risk a capital ship through the Dardanelles or the Aegean, as this would involve a very large escort which is much needed elsewhere. Churchill has suggested Alexandria or Jerusalem, and there is a possibility of Athens, though this is not yet sure.

In addition to this, I have, at the present time, a great hesitation in leaving here while my old Congress is in its final days, with the probability of its not final adjourning until the 15th of December. Furthermore, I am required by the Constitution to be here in order to send the annual message to the new Congress which meets here early in January.

My suggestion is that we should all meet about the 28th or 30th of January, and I should hope that by that time it will be possible for you to travel by rail to some Adriatic port and that we should meet you there or that you could come across in a few hours on one of our ships to Bari and then motor to Rome, or that you should take the same ship a little further in and that we should all meet at some place like Taormina, in Eastern Sicily, which at that time should provide a fairly good climate.

Almost any spot in the Mediterranean is accessible to me so that I can be within easy distances of Washington by air in order that I may carry out action on legislation—a subject you are familiar with. It must be possible for me to get bills or resolutions sent from here and returned within ten days. I hope that your January military operations will not prevent you from coming at that time, and I do not think that we should put off the meeting longer than to the end of January or early February.

If, of course, in the meantime, the Nazi army or people should disintegrate quickly, we should have to meet earlier, although I should much prefer that the meeting take place at the end of January.

Another suggestion is that the place of meeting should be one on the Riviera, but this would be dependent on withdrawal of the German troops from the northwestern part of Italy. I wish you would let me know your thoughts on this.

There are many things I hope to talk over with you. You and I understand each other's problems and, as you know, I like to keep these discussions informal, and I have no reason for formal agenda.

General Hurley, my Ambassador in China, is doing his best to iron out problems between the forces in Northern China and the Generalissimo. He is making some progress, but so far nothing has been signed.

I send you my warmest regards.

Personal and Secret from Premier J. V. Stalin to President F. Roosevelt

It is too bad that your naval authorities question the advisability of your original idea that the three of us should meet on the Soviet Black Sea coast. There is no objection, as far as I am concerned, to the time of meeting suggested by you—late January or early February; I expect, however, that we shall be able to select one of the Soviet seaports. I still have to pay heed to my doctors' warning of the risk involved in long journeys.

Even so, I hope that we shall be able to reach final agreement—a little later if not now—on a place acceptable to all of us.

Best wishes.

NOVEMBER 23, 1944

Most Secret and Personal from Premier J. V. Stalin to President F. Roosevelt

The indications are that de Gaulle and his friends, who have arrived in the Soviet Union, will raise two questions:

1. Concluding a Franco-Soviet pact of mutual aid similar to the Anglo-Soviet pact.

We shall find it hard to object. But I should like to know what you think. What do you advise?

2. De Gaulle will probably suggest revising the eastern frontier of France and shifting it to the left bank of the Rhine. There is talk, too, about a plan for forming a Rhine-Westphalian region under international control. Possibly French participation in the control is likewise envisaged. In other words, the French proposal for shifting the frontier line to the Rhine will compete with the plan for a Rhineland region under international control.

I would like your advice on this matter as well.

I have sent a similar message to Mr. Churchill.

DECEMBER 2, 1944

Received on December 7, 1944

Personal and Secret for Marshal Stalin from President Roosevelt

Many thanks for your two informative messages of December 2nd and 3rd.

With reference to a proposed Franco-Soviet pact along the lines of the Anglo-Soviet pact of mutual assistance, this Government would have no objection in principle if you and General de Gaulle considered such a pact in the interests of both your countries and European security generally.

With your replies to General de Gaulle regarding the postwar frontier of France, I am in complete agreement. At the present time, it appears to me that no advantage to our common war effort would result from an attempt to settle this question now, and that it is preferable that it be settled subsequent to the collapse of Germany.

Personal and Secret
from Premier J. V. Stalin
to the President, Mr. F. Roosevelt

The meeting with General de Gaulle provided the opportunity for a friendly exchange of views on Franco-Soviet relations. In the course of the talks, General de Gaulle, as I had anticipated, brought up two major issues: the French frontier on the Rhine and a Franco-Soviet mutual-aid pact patterned on the Anglo-Soviet Treaty.

As to the French frontier on the Rhine, I said, in effect, that the matter could not be settled without the knowledge and consent of our chief Allies, whose forces are waging a liberation struggle against the Germans on French soil. I stressed the difficulty of the problem.

Concerning the proposal for a Franco-Soviet mutual-aid pact, I pointed to the need for a thorough study of the matter and for clearing up the legal aspects, in particular the question of who in France, in the present circumstances, is to ratify such a pact. This means the French will have to offer a number of elucidations, which I have yet to receive from them.

I shall be obliged for a reply to this message and for your comments on these points.

I have sent a similar message to Mr. Churchill.

Best wishes.

DECEMBER 3, 1944

Personal and Secret from Premier J. V. Stalin to the Prime Minister, Mr. W. Churchill

Your message on Mikolajczyk received.

It has become obvious since my last meeting with Mr. Mikolajczyk in Moscow that he is incapable of helping a Polish settlement. Indeed, his negative role has been revealed. It is now evident that his negotiations with the Polish National Committee are designed to cover up those who, behind his back, engaged in criminal terror acts against Soviet officers and Soviet people generally on Polish territory. We cannot tolerate this state of affairs. We cannot tolerate terrorists, instigated by the Polish émigrés, assassinating our people in Poland and waging a criminal struggle against the Soviet forces liberating Poland. We look on these people as allies of our common enemy, and as to their radio correspondence with Mr Mikolajczyk, which we found on émigré agents arrested on Polish territory, it not only exposes their treacherous designs, it also casts a shadow on Mr Mikolajczyk and his men.

Ministerial changes in the émigré Government no longer deserve serious attention. For these elements, who have lost touch with the national soil and have no contact with their people, are merely marking time. Meanwhile the Polish Committee of National Liberation has made substantial progress in consolidating its national, democratic organizations on Polish soil, in implementing a land reform in favour of the peasants and in expanding its armed forces, and enjoys great prestige among the population.

I think that our task now is to support the National Committee in Lublin and all who want to cooperate and are capable of cooperating with it. This is particularly important to the Allies in view of the need for accelerating the defeat of the Germans.

DECEMBER 8, 1944

Received on December 14, 1944

Personal and Secret Message from President Roosevelt to Marshal Stalin

Since the prospects are still unsettled for an early meeting between us, and because of my conviction, in which I am confident you concur, that we must move forward as rapidly as possible in the convening of a general conference of the United Nations on the subject of an International Organization, I am requesting Ambassador Harriman to deliver this message and to discuss with you on my behalf the important subject of the voting procedure in the Security Council. Before the general conference will be possible, we will, of course, have to agree upon this and other questions. I am taking this matter up with Prime Minister Churchill as well.

I now feel, after giving this whole subject further consideration, that the substance of the following draft provision should be eminently satisfactory to everyone concerned.

Proposal for Section C of the Chapter on the Security Council:

Section C
Voting

1. One vote should be allotted to each member of the Security Council.

2. On matters of procedure, decisions of the Security Council should be made by an affirmative vote of seven members.

3. On all other matters, decisions of the Security Council should be made by an affirmative vote of seven members including the concurring votes of the permanent members; provided that a party to a dispute should abstain from voting in decisions under Chapter VIII, Section A, and under Paragraph One of Chapter VIII, Section C.

This calls, you will note, for the unanimity of the permanent members in all Council decisions relating to a determination of a threat to peace, as well as to action for the removal of such a threat or for the suppression of aggression or other breaches of the peace. As a practical matter, I can see that this is necessary if action of this kind is to be feasible. I am consequently prepared to accept in this respect the view expressed by your Government in its memorandum presented at the Dumbarton Oaks meetings on an International Security Organization. This naturally means that each permanent member would always have a vote in decisions of this character.

The Dumbarton Oaks proposals, at the same time, provide in Chapter VIII Section A for judicial or other procedures of a recommendatory character which may be employed by the Security Council in promoting voluntary peaceful settlement of disputes. In this respect, also, I am satisfied that if recommendations of the Security Council are concurred in by the permanent members, they will carry far greater weight. However, I am also convinced that such procedures will be effective only if the Great Powers exercise moral leadership by demonstrating their fidelity to the principles of justice. I firmly believe, therefore, that by accepting a provision under which all parties to a dispute would abstain from voting with regard to such procedures and thus indicating their willingness not to claim for themselves a special position in this respect, the permanent members would greatly enhance their moral prestige and would strengthen their own position as the principal guardians of the future peace, without jeopardizing in any way their vital interests or impairing the essential principle that the Great Powers must act unanimously in all decisions of the Council which affect such interests. To do this would make much more acceptable to all nations the overall plan, which must necessarily assign a special role to the Great Powers in the enforcement of peace.

Specific provisions for voting procedure on questions of this nature were not contained in either the Soviet or the American memoranda presented at Dumbarton Oaks. Our representatives there were not in a position, of course, to reach a definite agreement on this question. You and I must now find a way of completing the work which they have carried forward on our behalf so well.

Would you, if you are disposed to give favorable consideration to some such approach as I now suggest to the problem of voting in the Council, be willing that there be held as soon as possible a meeting of representatives designated by you, by me, and by Prime Minister Churchill to work out a complete provision on this question and to discuss the arrangements necessary for a prompt convening of a general conference of the United Nations?

Received on December 20, 1944

Personal and Secret for Marshal Stalin from President Roosevelt

I believe that, in view of the interest aroused in this country by Prime Minister Churchill's statement in the House of Commons yesterday and the strong pressure we are under to make known our position in regard to Poland, it may be necessary for this Government to issue some statement on the subject in the next few days. If issued, this statement will outline our attitude along the following lines:

(There followed the substance of the statement issued on December 18 by Mr. Stettinius, the full text of which is attached.)

As you will note, the proposed statement will, I am sure, contain nothing that is not known to you as the general attitude of this Government and, in so far as it goes, is I believe in general accord with the results of your discussion with Prime Minister Churchill in Moscow in the autumn and I am sure you will welcome it for this reason.

It is my feeling that it is of the highest importance that, until we three can get together and discuss this troublesome question thoroughly, there be no action on any side which would render our discussions more difficult.

I have seen indications that the Lublin Committee may be intending to give itself the status of a Provisional Government of Poland. I appreciate fully the desirability from your point of view of having a clarification of Polish authority before your armies move further into Poland. However, because of the great political implications which such a step would entail, I very much hope that you would find it possible to refrain from recognizing the Lublin Committee as a Government of Poland before we meet, which I hope will be immediately after my inauguration on January 20. Could you not continue to deal with the Committee in its present form until that date? I know that my views on this point are shared by Prime Minister Churchill.

STATEMENT BY Mr. STETTINIUS
Issued on December 18, 1944

The United States Government stands unequivocally for a strong, free and independent Polish state with the untrammeled right of the Polish people to order their internal existence as they see fit.

It has been the consistently held policy of the United States Government that questions relating to boundaries should be left in abeyance until the termination of hostilities. As Mr.

Hull stated in his address of April 9, 1944, "this does not mean that certain questions may not and should not in the meantime be settled by friendly conferences and agreement." In the case of the future frontiers of Poland, if a mutual agreement is reached by the United Nations directly concerned, this Government would have no objection to such an agreement which could make an essential contribution to the prosecution of the war against the common enemy. If, as a result of such agreement, the Government and people of Poland decide that it would be in the interests of the Polish state to transfer national groups, the United States Government, in co-operation with other governments, will assist Poland, in so far as practicable, in such transfers. The United States Government continues to adhere to its traditional policy of declining to give guarantees for any specific frontiers. The United States Government is working for the establishment of a world security organization through which the United States together with other member states would assume responsibility for the preservation of general security.

It is the announced aim of the United States Government, subject to legislative authority, to assist the countries liberated from the enemy in repairing the devastation of war and thus to bring to their peoples the opportunity to join as full partners in the task of building a more prosperous and secure life for all men and women. This applies to Poland as well as the other United Nations.

The policy of the United States Government regarding Poland outlined above has as its objective the attainment of the announced basic principles of the United States foreign policy.

Personal and Secret for Marshal Stalin from President Roosevelt

I must tell you that I am disturbed and deeply disappointed by your message of December 27 regarding Poland in which you tell me that you cannot see your way clear to hold the question of recognition of the Lublin Committee as the Provisional Government in abeyance until we have had an opportunity to discuss thoroughly the whole question at our meeting. I would have thought that no serious inconvenience would have been caused your Government or your Armies if you were to delay the purely juridical act of recognition for the short period of a month remaining until our meeting. In my request there was no suggestion that you curtail your practical relations with the Lublin Committee, nor any thought that you should deal with or accept the London Government in its present composition. I had urged this delay upon you because of my feeling that you would realize how extremely unfortunate and even serious it would be in its effect on world opinion and enemy morale at this time in the war if your Government should formally recognize one Government of Poland while the majority of the other United Nations, including Great Britain and the United States, continue to recognize the Polish Government in London and maintain diplomatic relations with it.

With frankness equal to your own, I must tell you that I see no prospect of this Government's following suit and transferring its recognition from the London Government to the Lublin Committee in its present form. In no sense is this due to any special ties or feelings for the Government in London. The fact is that as yet neither the Government nor the people of the United States have seen any evidence arising either from the manner of its creation or from subsequent developments to justify the conclusion that the Lublin Committee, as at present constituted, represents the people of Poland. I cannot ignore the fact that only a small fraction of Poland proper, west of the Curzon Line, has yet been liberated from German tyranny, and it is therefore an unquestioned truth that no opportunity to express themselves in regard to the Lublin Committee has been afforded the people of Poland.

If there is established at some future date following the liberation of Poland a Provisional Government of Poland with popular support, the attitude of this Government would, of course, be governed by the Polish people's decision.

I share fully your opinion that the situation has been worsened by the departure of Mr. Mikolajczyk from the Government in London. I have always felt that Mr. Mikolajczyk, who I am convinced is sincerely desirous of settling all points at issue between the Soviet Union and Poland, is the only Polish leader in sight who seems to offer the possibility of a genuine solution of the difficult and dangerous Polish question. From my personal knowledge of Mr. Mikolajczyk and my conversations with him when he was here in Washington and his subsequent efforts and policies during his visit at Moscow, I find it most difficult to believe that he had knowledge of any instructions for acts of terrorism.

This message is sent to you so that you will know this Government's position regarding the recognition at the present time of the Lublin Committee as the Provisional Government of Poland. I am more than ever convinced that when the three of us meet, we can reach a solution of the Polish problem, and I therefore still hope that you can hold the formal recognition of the Lublin Committee as a Government of Poland in abeyance until then. I cannot see any great objection to a month's delay from a military angle.

Personal and Secret
from Premier J. V. Stalin
to the President, Mr. F. Roosevelt

Your message reached me through Mr. Harriman on December 14.

I fully share your opinion that before the general conference of the United Nations meets to discuss the founding of an International Organization, it would be advisable for us to reach agreement on the more important problems that found no solution at Dumbarton Oaks, primarily on the voting procedure in the Security Council. I feel it necessary to recall that the original American draft stressed the necessity of drawing up special rules with regard to voting procedure in the event of a dispute directly affecting one of several permanent members of the Council. The British draft, too, pointed out that the general procedure of settling disputes between the Great Powers, should disputes arise, might prove unworkable.

In this connection, paragraphs 1 and 2 of your proposal do not give rise to any objections and can be accepted, it being understood that paragraph 2 is concerned with questions of procedure mentioned in Chapter VI, Section D.

As to paragraph 3 of your proposal, I regret to say that I cannot accept it as worded by you. As acknowledged by you, the principle of unanimity of the permanent members is indispensable in all Council decisions determining a threat to peace, as well as in those calling for action to remove the threat or to crush aggression or other breaches of peace. In adopting decisions on these questions there should, without doubt, be complete agreement among the Powers who [sic] are permanent members of the Council and bear the chief responsibility for the maintenance of peace and security. It goes without saying that any attempt to bar, at any stage, one or several permanent members of the Council from voting on the questions mentioned above, and this, theoretically speaking, is possible, and it may even be that the majority of the permanent members find themselves excluded from participation in settling an issue—could have dire consequences for the preservation of international security. This runs counter to the principle of agreement and unanimity in the decisions of the four leading Powers and may result in some of the Great Powers being played against others—a development which would be likely to undermine universal security. The small countries are interested in preventing that just as much as the Great Powers, for a split among the Great Powers [sic] have united to safeguard peace and the security of all freedom-loving nations is fraught with the most dangerous consequences to all those states.

That is why I must insist on our former stand as to the voting in the Security Council. As I see it, this attitude will ensure four-Power unity for the new International Organization and help to prevent attempts at playing some of the Great Powers against others, which is vital to their joint struggle against future aggression. Such a situation would, naturally, safeguard the interests of the small nations in maintaining their security and would be in keeping with the interests of universal peace.

I hope that you will fully appreciate the importance of the considerations set forth above in support of the principle of unanimity of the four leading Powers and that we shall arrive at agreed decisions on this point, as well as on certain other points still outstanding. On the basis of an agreed decision, our representative could work out a final draft and discuss the measures necessary for the early convening of a general United Nations conference.

DECEMBER 26, 1944

Personal and Secret
from Premier J. V. Stalin
to the President, Mr. F. Roosevelt

Your message on Polish affairs reached me on December 20.

As to Mr. Stettinius' statement of December 18, I should prefer to comment on it when we meet. At any rate events in Poland have already gone far beyond that which is reflected in the said statement.

A number of things that have taken place since Mr. Mikolajczyk's last visit to Moscow, in particular the wireless correspondence with the Mikolajczyk Government, which we found on terrorists arrested in Poland—underground agents of the émigré Government—demonstrate beyond all doubt that Mr. Mikolajczyk's talks with the Polish National Committee served to cover up those elements who, behind Mr. Mikolajczyk's back, had been engaged in terror against Soviet officers and soldiers in Poland. We cannot tolerate a situation in which terrorists, instigated by Polish émigrés, assassinate Red Army soldiers and officers in Poland, wage a criminal struggle against the Soviet forces engaged in liberating Poland and directly aid our enemies, with whom they are virtually in league. The substitution of Arciszewski for Mikolajczyk and the ministerial changes in the émigré Government in general have aggravated the situation and have resulted in a deep rift between Poland and the émigré Government.

Meanwhile the National Committee has made notable progress in consolidating the Polish state and the machinery of state power on Polish soil, in expanding and strengthening the Polish Army, in implementing a number of important government measures, primarily the land reform in favour of the peasants. These developments have resulted in the consolidation of the democratic forces in Poland and in an appreciable increase in the prestige of the National Committee among the Polish people and large sections of the Poles abroad.

As I see it, we must now be interested in supporting the National Committee and all who are willing to cooperate and who are capable of cooperating with it, which is of special moment for the Allies and for fulfilment of our common task —accelerating the defeat of Hitler Germany. For the Soviet Union, which is bearing the whole burden of the struggle for freeing Poland from the German invaders, the problem of relations with Poland is, in present circumstances, a matter of everyday, close and friendly relations with an authority brought into being by the Polish people on their own soil, an authority which has already grown strong and has armed forces of its own, which, together with the Red Army, are fighting the Germans.

I must say frankly that in the event of the Polish Committee of National Liberation becoming a Provisional Polish Government, the Soviet Government will, in view of the foregoing, have no serious reasons for postponing its recognition. It should be borne in mind that the Soviet Union, more than any other Power, has a stake in strengthening a pro-Ally and democratic Poland, not only because she is bearing the brunt of the struggle for Poland's liberation, but also because Poland borders on the Soviet Union and because the Polish problem is inseparable from that of the security of the Soviet Union. To this I should add that the Red Army's success in fighting the Germans in Poland largely depends on a tranquil and reliable rear in Poland, and the Polish National Committee is fully cognisant of this circumstance, whereas the émigré Government and its underground agents by their acts of terror threaten civil war in the rear of the Red Army and counter its successes.

On the other hand, in the conditions now prevailing in Poland there are no grounds for continuing to support the émigré Government, which has completely forfeited the trust of the population inside the country and which, moreover, threatens civil war in the rear of the Red Army, thereby injuring our common interest in the success of the struggle we are waging against the Germans. I think it would be only natural, fair and beneficial to our common cause if the Governments of the Allied Powers agreed as a first step to exchange representatives at this juncture with the National Committee with a view to its later recognition as the lawful government of Poland, after it has proclaimed itself the Provisional Government of Poland. Unless this is done I fear that the Polish people's trust in the Allied Powers may diminish. I think we should not countenance a situation in which Poles can say that we are sacrificing the interests of Poland to those of a handful of émigrés in London.

DECEMBER 27, 1944

PART V

1945

Personal and Secret
from Premier J. V. Stalin
to the President, Mr. F. Roosevelt

Your message of December 27 recieved.

I am very sorry that I have not succeeded in convincing you of the correctness of the Soviet Government's stand on the Polish question. Nevertheless, I hope events will convince you that the National Committee has always given important help to the Allies, and continues to do so, particularly, to the Red Army, in the struggle against Hitler Germany, while the émigré Government in London is disorganizing that struggle, thereby helping the Germans.

Of course I quite understand your proposal for postponing recognition of the Provisional Government of Poland by the Soviet Union for a month. But one circumstance makes me powerless to comply with your wish. The point is that on December 27 the Presidium of the Supreme Soviet of the U.S.S.R., replying to a corresponding question by the Poles, declared that it would recognize the Provisional Government of Poland the moment it was set up. This circumstance makes me powerless to comply with your wish.

Allow me to congratulate you on the New Year and to wish you good health and success.

JANUARY 1, 1945

Personal and Secret
from Premier J. V. Stalin
to the Prime Minister,
Mr. W. Churchill

You, no doubt, know already that the Polish National Council in Lublin has announced its decision to transform the National Committee into a Provisional National Government of the Polish Republic. You are well aware of our attitude to the National Committee, which, in our view, has already won great prestige in Poland and is the lawful exponent of the will of the Polish people. The decision to make it the Provisional Government seems to us quite timely, especially now that Mikolajczyk has withdrawn from the émigré Government and that the latter has thereby lost all semblance of a government. I think that Poland cannot be left without a government. Accordingly, the Soviet Government has agreed to recognise the Provisional Polish Government.

I greatly regret that I have not succeeded in fully convincing you of the correctness of the Soviet Government's stand on the Polish question. Still, I hope the events will show that our recognition of the Polish Government in Lublin is in keeping with the interests of the common cause of the Allies and that it will help accelerate the defeat of Germany.

I enclose for your information the two messages I sent to the President on the Polish question.

2. I know that the President has your consent to a meeting of the three of us at the end of the month or early in February. I shall be glad to see you both on our soil and hope that our joint work will be a success.

I take this opportunity to send you New Year greetings and to wish you the best of health and success.

J A N U A R Y 3 , 1 9 4 5

Personal and Most Secret Message from Mr. Churchill to Marshal Stalin

Your personal and secret message of January 3rd, 1945.

I thank you for sending me your two messages to the President on the Polish question. Naturally I and my War Cabinet colleagues are distressed at the course events are taking. I am quite clear that much the best thing is for us three to meet together and talk all these matters over, not only as isolated problems but in relation to the whole world situation both of war and transit to peace. Meanwhile, our attitude, as you know it, remains unchanged.

2. I look forward very much to this momentous meeting and I am glad that the President of the United States has been willing to make this long journey. We have agreed, subject to your concurrence, that the code name shall be called "Argonaut" and I hope that you will use that in any messages that may be interchanged by the staffs who will be consulting about arrangements.

3. I have just come back from General Eisenhower's and Field Marshal Montgomery's separate headquarters. The battle in Belgium is very heavy but it is thought that we have the mastery. The dispersionary attack which the Germans are making into Alsace also causes difficulties with the French and tends to pin down American forces. I still remain of the opinion that weight and weapons, including air, of the Allied forces will make von Rundstedt regret his daring and well organised attempt to split our front and, if possible, lay hands on the now absolutely vital Antwerp port.

4. I reciprocate your cordial wishes for the New Year. May it shorten the agony of the great nations we serve and bring about a lasting peace on our joint guarantee.

J A N U A R Y 5 t h , 1 9 4 5

Personal and Most Secret Message from Mr. Churchill to Marshal Stalin

The battle in the West is very heavy and, at any time, large decisions may be called for from the Supreme Command. You know yourself from your own experience how very anxious the position is when a very broad front has to be defended after temporary loss of the initiative. It is General Eisenhower's great desire and need to know in outline what you plan to do, as this obviously affects all his and our major decisions. Our Envoy, Air Chief Marshal Tedder, was last night reported weather-bound in Cairo. His journey has been much delayed through no fault of yours. In case he has not reached you yet, I shall be grateful if you can tell me whether we can count on a major Russian offensive on the Vistula front, or elsewhere, during January, with any other points you may care to mention. I shall not pass this most secret information to anyone except Field Marshal Brooke and General Eisenhower, and only under conditions of the utmost secrecy. I regard the matter as urgent.

JANUARY 6TH, 1945

Personal and Most Secret from Premier J. V. Stalin to the Prime Minister, Mr. W. Churchill

Your message of January 6 reached me in the evening of January 7.

I am sorry to say that Air Marshal Tedder has not yet arrived in Moscow.

It is extremely important to take advantage of our superiority over the Germans in guns and aircraft. What we need for the purpose is clear flying weather and the absence of low mists that prevent aimed artillery fire. We are mounting an offensive, but at the moment the weather is unfavourable. Still, in view of our Allies' position on the Western Front, GHQ of the Supreme Command have decided to complete preparations at a rapid rate and, regardless of weather, to launch large-scale offensive operations along the entire Central Front not later than the second half of January. Rest assured we shall do all in our power to support the valiant forces of our Allies.

J A N U A R Y   7 ,   1 9 4 5

Personal and Most Secret from Premier J. V. Stalin to the President, Mr. F. Roosevelt

Today, January 15, I had a talk with Marshal Tedder and the generals accompanying him. In my view, the information we exchanged was complete enough. Both parties gave exhaustive answers to the questions. I must say that I was most impressed by Marshal Tedder.

After four days of offensive operations on the Soviet-German front, I am now in a position to inform you that our offensive is making satisfactory progress despite unfavorable weather. The entire Central Front—from the Carpathians to the Baltic Sea—is moving westwards. The Germans, though resisting desperately, are retreating. I reel sure that they will have to disperse their reserves between the two fronts and, as a result, relinquish the offensive on the Western Front. I am glad that this circumstance will ease the position of the Allied troops in the West and expedite preparations for the offensive planned by General Eisenhower.

As regards the Soviet troops, you may rest assured that, despite the difficulties, they will do all in their power to make the blow as effective as possible.

JANUARY 15, 1945

Received on January 18, 1945

Personal and Top Secret
for Marshal Stalin
from President Roosevelt

Many thanks for your encouraging message of January 15 regarding your conference with Air Marshal Tedder and the offensive of your armies on the Soviet-German front.

Your heroic soldiers' past performance and the efficiency they have already demonstrated in this offensive give high promise of an early success to our armies on both fronts. The time required to force surrender upon our barbarian enemies will be radically reduced by skillful coordination of our combined efforts.

America, as you know, is putting forth a great effort in the Pacific at a distance of seven thousand miles, and my hope is that an early collapse of Germany will permit the movement to the Pacific area of sufficient forces to destroy quickly the menace of Japan to all of our Allies.

Marshal J. V. Stalin

Koreiz, the Crimea

My dear Marshal Stalin,

I have been giving a great deal of thought to our meeting this afternoon, and I want to tell you, in all frankness, what is on my mind.

In so far as the Polish Government is concerned, I am greatly disturbed that the three Great Powers do not have a meeting of minds about the political set-up in Poland. It seems to me that it puts all of us in a bad light throughout the world to have you recognizing one government while we and the British are recognizing another in London. I am sure this state of affairs should not continue and that if it does it can only lead our people to think there is a breach between us, which is not the case. I am determined that there shall be no breach between ourselves and the Soviet Union. Surely there is a way to reconcile our differences.

I was very much impressed with some of the things you said today, particularly your determination that your rear must be safeguarded as your army moves into Berlin. You cannot, and we must not, tolerate any temporary government which will give your armed forces any trouble of this sort. I want you to know that I am fully mindful of this.

You must believe me when I tell you that our people at home look with a critical eye on what they consider a disagreement between us at this vital stage of the war. They, in effect, say that if we cannot get a meeting of minds now, when our armies are converging on the common enemy, how can we get an understanding on even more vital things in the future.

I have had to make it clear to you that we cannot recognize the Lublin Government as now composed, and the world would regard it as a lamentable outcome of our work here if we parted with an open and obvious divergence between us on this issue.

You said today that you would be prepared to support any suggestions for the solution of this problem which offered a fair chance of success, and you also mentioned the possibility of bringing some members of the Lublin Government here.

Realizing that we all have the same anxiety in getting this matter settled, I would like to develop your proposal a little and suggest that we invite here to Yalta at once Mr. Beirut and Mr. Osubka Morawski from the Lublin Government and also two or three from the following list of Poles, which, according to our information, would be desirable as representatives of the other elements of the Polish people in the development of a new temporary government which all three of us could recognize and support: Bishop Sapieha of Cracow, Vincente Witos, Mr. Zurlowski, Professor Buyak, and Professor Kutzeba. If, as a result of the presence of these Polish leaders here, we could jointly agree with them on a provisional government in Poland which should no doubt include some Polish leaders from abroad, such as Mr. Mikolajczyk, Mr. Grabski, and Mr. Romer, the United States Government, and I feel sure the British Government as well, would then be prepared to examine with you conditions in which they would dissociate themselves from the London government and transfer their recognition to the new provisional government.

I hope I do not have to assure you that the United States will never lend its support in any way to any provisional government in Poland that would be inimical to your interests.

It goes without saying that any interim government which could be formed as a result of our conference with the Poles here would be pledged to the holding of free elections in Poland at the earliest possible date. I know this is completely consistent with your desire to see a new free and democratic Poland emerge from the welter of this war.

> *Most sincerely yours,*
> *Franklin D. ROOSEVELT*

FEBRUARY 6, 1945

Marshal J. V. Stalin

Koreiz, the Crimea

My dear Marshal Stalin,

I have been thinking, as I must, of possible political difficulties which I might encounter in the United States in connection with the number of votes which the Big Powers will
enjoy in the Assembly of the World Organization. We have
agreed, and I shall certainly carry out that agreement, to support, at the forthcoming United Nations Conference, the admission of the Ukrainian and White Russian Republics as
members of the Assembly of the World Organization. I am
somewhat concerned lest it be pointed out that the United
States will have only one vote in the Assembly. It may be
necessary for me, therefore, if I am to ensure wholehearted
acceptance by the Congress and people of the United States of
our participation in the World Organization, to ask for additional votes in the Assembly in order to give parity to the
United States.

I would like to know, before I face this problem, that you
would perceive no objection and would support a proposal
along this line if it is necessary for me to make it at the forthcoming conference. I would greatly appreciate your letting me
have your views in reply to this letter.

Most sincerely yours,
Franklin D. ROOSEVELT

FEBRUARY 10, 1945

To President Franklin D. Roosevelt

"Livadia," the Crimea

My dear Mr. Roosevelt,
   Your letter of February 10 received. I fully agree with you that because the Soviet Union's votes will increase to three owing to the admission of the Soviet Ukraine and Soviet Byelorussia to Assembly membership, the number of U.S. votes should likewise be increased.
   I think that the U.S. votes should be raised to three as in the case of the Soviet Union and its two main republics. If necessary, I am prepared to give official endorsement to this proposal.

Most sincerely yours,
J. STALIN

KOREIZ, FEBRUARY 11, 1945

Received on February 13, 1945

Personal and Secret for Marshal Stalin from President Roosevelt

I wish again, upon leaving the hospitable shores of the Soviet Union, to tell you how deeply grateful I am for the many kindnesses which you showed me while I was your guest in the Crimea. I leave greatly heartened as a result of the meeting between you, the Prime Minister, and myself. The peoples of the world, I am sure, will regard the achievements of this meeting not only with approval, but as a genuine assurance that our three great nations can work in peace as well as they have in war.

Received on February 23, 1945

His Excellency Joseph V. Stalin, Supreme Commander of the Armed Forces of the Union of Soviet Socialist Republics

Moscow

In anticipation of our common victory against the Nazi oppressors, I wish to take this opportunity to extend my heartiest congratulations to you as Supreme Commander on this, the twenty-seventh anniversary of the founding of the Red Army. The far-reaching decisions we took at Yalta will hasten victory and the establishment of a firm foundation for a lasting peace. The continued outstanding achievements of the Red Army, together with the all-out effort of the United Nations forces in the South and the West, assure the speedy attainment of our common goal: a peaceful world based upon mutual understanding and cooperation.

Franklin D. ROOSEVELT

Received on February 18, 1945

Message from Mr. Churchill
to Marshal Stalin

On behalf of His Majesty's Government I send you grateful thanks for all the hospitality and friendship extended to the British delegation to the Crimea Conference. We were deeply impressed by the feats of organisation and of improvisation which enabled the Conference to meet in such agreeable and imposing surroundings, and we all take back with us most happy recollections. To this I must add a personal expression of my own thanks and gratitude. No previous meeting has shown so clearly the results which can be achieved when the three heads of Government meet together with the firm intention to face difficulties and solve them. You yourself said that cooperation would be less easy when the unifying bond of the fight against a common enemy had been removed. I am resolved, as I am sure the President and you are resolved, that the friendship and cooperation so firmly established shall not fade when victory has been won. I pray that you may long be spared to preside over the destinies of your country which has shown its full greatness under your leadership, and I send you my best wishes and heartfelt thanks.

F E B R U A R Y   1 7 T H ,   1 9 4 5

Received on March 4, 1945

Personal and Secret for Marshal Stalin from President Roosevelt

I have reliable information regarding the difficulties which are being encountered in collecting, supplying, and evacuating American ex-prisoners of war and American aircraft crews who are stranded east of the Russian lines. It is urgently requested that instructions be issued authorizing ten American aircraft with American crews to operate between Poltava and places in Poland where American ex-prisoners of war and stranded airmen may be located. This authority is requested for the purpose of providing supplementary clothing, medical, and food supplies for all American soldiers, to evacuate stranded aircraft crews and liberated prisoners of war, and especially to transfer the injured and sick to the American hospital at Poltava. I regard this request to be of the greatest importance not only for humanitarian reasons, but also by reason of the intense interest of the American public in the welfare of our ex-prisoners of war and stranded aircraft crews.

Secondly, on the general matter of prisoners of war still in German hands, I feel that we ought to do something quickly. The number of these prisoners of war—Russian, British and United States—is very large. In view of your disapproval of the plan we submitted, what do you suggest instead?

Personal and Secret
from Premier J. V. Stalin
to the President, Mr. F. Roosevelt

Your message of March 4 about prisoners of war received.
I have again conferred with our local representatives in charge
of this matter and can tell you the following:

The difficulties which arose during the early stages of the
speedy evacuation of American prisoners of war from the
zones of direct military operations have decreased substantially. At present the special agency set up by the Soviet Government to take care of foreign prisoners of war has adequate
personnel, transport facilities, and food supplies, and whenever new groups of American prisoners of war are discovered,
steps are taken at once to help them and to evacuate them to
assembly points for subsequent repatriation. According to the
information available to the Soviet Government, there is now
no accumulation of U.S. prisoners of war on Polish territory
or in other areas liberated by the Red Army, because all of
them, with the exception of individual sick men who are in
hospital, have been sent to the assembly point in Odessa,
where 1,200 U.S. prisoners of war have arrived so far and the
arrival of the remainder is expected shortly. Hence there is no
need at the moment for U.S. planes to fly from Poltava to
Polish territory in connection with U.S. prisoners of war. You
may rest assured that appropriate measures will immediately
be taken also with regard to American aircraft crews making a
forced landing. This, however, does not rule out cases in
which the help of U.S. aircraft may be required. In this event,
the Soviet military authorities will request the U.S. military
representatives in Moscow to send U.S. aircraft from Poltava.

As at the moment I have no proposals to make concerning the status of the Allied prisoners of war in German hands, I should like to assure you that we shall do all we can to provide them with facilities as soon as they find themselves on territory captured by Soviet troops.

MARCH 5, 1945

Personal and Secret
from Premier J. V. Stalin
to the President, Mr. F. Roosevelt

I am in receipt of your message about the evacuation of former U.S. prisoners of war from Poland.

With regard to your information about allegedly large numbers of sick and injured Americans in Poland or awaiting evacuation to Odessa, or who have not contacted the Soviet authorities, I must say that the information is inaccurate. Actually, apart from a certain number who are on their way to Odessa, there were only 17 sick U.S. servicemen on Polish soil as of March 16. I have today received a report which says that the 17 men will be flown to Odessa in a few days.

With reference to the request contained in your message, I must say that if it concerned me personally, I would be ready to give way even to the detriment of my own interests. But, in the given instance, the matter concerns the interests of Soviet armies at the front and of Soviet commanders who do not want to have around odd officers who, while having no relation to the military operations, need looking after, want all kinds of meetings and contacts, protection against possible acts of sabotage by German agents not yet ferreted out, and other things that divert the attention of the commanders and their subordinates from their direct duties. Our commanders bear full responsibility for the state of affairs at the front and in the immediate rear, and I do not see how I can restrict their rights to any extent.

I must also say that U.S. ex-prisoners of war liberated by the Red Army have been treated to good conditions in Soviet camps—better conditions than those afforded Soviet ex-prisoners of war in U.S. camps, where some of them were lodged with German war prisoners and were subjected to unfair treatment and unlawful persecutions, including beating, as has been communicated to the U.S. Government on more than one occasion.

MARCH 22, 1945

———

Received on March 25, 1945

Personal and Top Secret for Marshal Stalin from President Roosevelt

Ambassador Harriman has communicated to me a letter which he has received from Mr. Molotov regarding an investigation being made by Field Marshal Alexander into a reported possibility of obtaining the surrender of part or all of the German army in Italy. In this letter Mr. Molotov demands that, because of the nonparticipation therein of Soviet officers, this investigation to be undertaken in Switzerland should be stopped forthwith.

The facts of this matter I am sure have, through a misunderstanding, not been correctly presented to you. The following are the facts:

Unconfirmed information was received some days ago in Switzerland that some German officers were considering the possibility of arranging for the surrender of German troops that are opposed to Field Marshal Alexander's British-American Armies in Italy.

Upon the receipt of this information in Washington, Field Marshal Alexander was authorized to send to Switzerland an officer or officers of his staff to ascertain the accuracy of the report, and if it appeared to be of sufficient promise, to arrange with any competent German officers for a conference to discuss details of the surrender with Field Marshal Alexander at his headquarters in Italy. If such a meeting could be arranged, Soviet representatives would, of course, be welcome.

Information concerning this investigation to be made in Switzerland was immediately communicated to the Soviet Government. Your Government was later informed that it will be agreeable for Soviet officers to be present at Field Marshal Alexander's meetings with German officers if and when arrangements are finally made in Berne for such a meeting at Caserta to discuss details of a surrender.

Up to the present time, the attempts by our representatives to arrange a meeting with German officers have met with no success, but it still appears that such a meeting is a possibility.

My Government, as you will of course understand, must give every assistance to all officers in the field in command of Allied forces who believe there is a possibility of forcing the surrender of enemy troops in their area. For me to take any other attitude or to permit any delay which must cause additional and avoidable loss of life in the American forces would be completely unreasonable. As a military man, you will understand the necessity for prompt action to avoid losing an opportunity. The sending of a flag of truce to your General at Königsberg or Danzig would be in the same category.

There can be, in such a surrender of enemy forces in the field, no violation of our agreed principle of unconditional surrender and no political implications whatever.

I will be pleased to have, at any discussion of the details of surrender by our commander of American forces in the field, the benefit of the experience and advice of any of your officers who can be present, but I cannot agree to suspend investigation of the possibility because of objection by Mr.

Molotov for some reason completely beyond my comprehension.

Not much is expected from the reported possibility, but for the purpose of preventing misunderstanding between our officers, I hope you will point out to the Soviet officials concerned, the desirability and necessity of our taking prompt and effective action without any delay to effect the surrender of any enemy military forces that are opposed to American forces in the field.

I feel certain that you will have the same attitude and will take the same action when a similar opportunity comes on the Soviet front.

———————

Received on March 25, 1945

Personal and Secret for Marshal Stalin from President Roosevelt

The State Department has just been informed by Ambassador Gromyko concerning the composition of the Soviet Delegation to the San Francisco Conference. We have the highest regard for Ambassador Gromyko's character and capabilities and know that he would ably represent the Soviet Union. Nevertheless, I cannot help but be deeply disappointed that Mr. Molotov apparently does not plan to attend. Recalling the friendly and fruitful cooperation at Yalta between Mr. Molotov, Mr. Eden, and Mr. Stettinius, I know that the Secretary of State has been looking forward to continuing at San Francisco in the same spirit the joint work for the eventual realization of our common goal: the establishment of an effective international organization to ensure for the world a secure and peaceful future.

The Conference, without Mr. Molotov's presence, will be deprived of a very great asset. If his pressing and heavy responsibilities in the Soviet Union make it impossible for him to stay for the entire Conference, I hope very much that you will find it possible to let him come at least for the vital opening sessions. All sponsoring Powers and the majority of the other countries attending will be represented by their Ministers of Foreign Affairs. In these circumstances, I am afraid that Mr. Molotov's absence will be construed all over the world as a lack of comparable interest in the great objectives of this Conference on the part of the Soviet Government.

Personal and Secret from Premier J. V. Stalin to the President, Mr. F. Roosevelt

I have analyzed the matter raised in your letter of March 25, and find that the Soviet Government could not have given any other reply after its representatives were barred from the Berne negotiations with the Germans for a German surrender and opening the front to the Anglo-American troops in Northern Italy.

Far from being against, I am all for profiting from cases of disintegration in the German armies to hasten their surrender on one or another sector and encourage them to open the front to Allied forces.

But I agree to such talks with the enemy only in cases

where they do not lead to an easing of the enemy's position, if the opportunity for the Germans to maneuver and to use the talks for switching troops to other sectors, above all to the Soviet front, is precluded.

And it was solely with an eye to providing this guarantee that the Soviet Government found it necessary to have representatives of its Military Command take part in such negotiations with the enemy wherever they might take place—whether in Berne or in Caserta. I cannot understand why the representatives of the Soviet Command have been excluded from the talks and in what way they could have handicapped the representatives of the Allied Command.

I must tell you for your information that the Germans have already taken advantage of the talks with the Allied Command to move three divisions from Northern Italy to the Soviet front.

The task of coordinated operations involving a blow at the Germans from the West, South and East, proclaimed at the Crimea Conference, is to hold the enemy on the spot and prevent him from maneuvering, from moving his forces to the points where he needs them most. The Soviet Command is doing this. But Field Marshal Alexander is not. This circumstance irritates the Soviet Command and engenders distrust.

"As a military man," you write to me, "you will understand the necessity for prompt action to avoid losing an opportunity. The sending of a flag of truce to your General at Königsberg or Danzig would be in the same category." I am afraid the analogy does not fit the case. The German troops at Danzig and at Königsberg are encircled. If they surrender, they will do so to escape extermination, but they cannot open the front to Soviet troops because the front has shifted as far west as the Oder. The German troops in Northern Italy are in an entirely different position. They are not encircled and are not faced with extermination. If, nevertheless, the Germans in Northern Italy seek negotiations in order to surrender and to open the front to the Allied troops, then they must have some other, more far-reaching aims affecting the destiny of Germany.

I must tell you that if a similar situation had obtained on the Eastern Front, somewhere on the Oder, providing an opportunity for a German surrender and for the opening of the front to the Soviet troops, I should have immediately notified the Anglo-American Military Command and asked it to send its representatives to take part in the talks, for in a situation of this kind Allies should have nothing to conceal from each other.

MARCH 29, 1945

Received on April 1, 1945

Personal and Top Secret
for Marshal Stalin
from President Roosevelt

In the exchange of messages we have had on possible future negotiations with the Germans for surrender of their forces in Italy, it seems to me that, although both of us are in agreement on all the basic principles, the matter now stands in an atmosphere of regrettable apprehension and mistrust.

No negotiations for surrender have been entered into, and if there should be any negotiations, they will be conducted at Caserta with your representatives present throughout. Although the attempt at Berne to arrange for the conduct of these negotiations has been fruitless, Marshal Alexander has been directed to keep you informed of his progress in this matter.

I must repeat that the meeting in Berne was for the single purpose of arranging contact with competent German military officers and not for negotiations of any kind.

There is no question of negotiating with the Germans in

any way which would permit them to transfer elsewhere forces from the Italian front. Negotiations, if any are conducted, will be on the basis of unconditional surrender. With regard to the lack of Allied offensive operations in Italy, this condition has in no way resulted from any expectation of an agreement with the Germans. As a matter of fact, recent interruption of offensive operations in Italy has been due primarily to the recent transfer of Allied forces, British and Canadian divisions, from that front to France. Preparations are now made for an offensive on the Italian front about April 10, but while we hope for success, the operation will be of limited power due to the lack of forces now available to Alexander. He has seventeen dependable divisions and is opposed by twenty-four German divisions. We intend to do everything within the capacity of our available resources to prevent any withdrawal of the German forces now in Italy.

I feel that your information about the time of the movements of German troops from Italy is in error. Our best information is that three German divisions have left Italy since the first of the year, two of which have gone to the Eastern Front. The last division of the three started moving about February 25, more than two weeks before anybody heard of any possibility of a surrender. It is therefore clearly evident that the approach made of German agents in Berne occurred after the last movement of troops began and could not possibly have had any effect on the movement.

This entire episode has arisen through the initiative of a German officer reputed to be close to Himmler and there is, of course, a strong possibility that his sole purpose is to create suspicion and distrust between the Allies. There is no reason why we should permit him to succeed in that aim. I trust that the above categorical statement of the present situation and of my intentions will allay the apprehension which you express in your message of March 29.

Personal and Secret
from Marshal J. V. Stalin
to the President, Mr. F. Roosevelt

We highly value and attach great importance to the San Francisco Conference to lay the foundations of an international organization for peace and security of the nations, but present circumstances preclude V. M. Molotov's attendence. I and Molotov are very sorry about this, but the convening, at the insistence of Deputies to the Supreme Soviet, of a session of the Supreme Soviet of the U.S.S.R. in April, at which Molotov's attendance is imperative, makes it impossible for him to attend even the opening session of the Conference.

You are aware that Ambassador Gromyko successfully coped with his task at Dumbarton Oaks, and we are certain that he will ably head the Soviet Delegation at San Francisco.

As to the different interpretations, you will appreciate that they cannot determine the decisions to be taken.

MARCH 27, 1945

Received on April 1, 1945

Personal and Top Secret
for Marshal Stalin
from President Roosevelt

I cannot conceal from you the concern with which I view
the developments of events of mutual interest since our fruitful
meeting at Yalta. The decisions we reached there were good
ones and have, for the most part, been welcomed with enthusiasm by the peoples of the world who saw in our ability to
find a common basis of understanding the best pledge for a
secure and peaceful world after this war. Precisely because of
the hopes and expectations that these decisions raised, their
fulfillment is being followed with the closest attention. We
have no right to let them be disappointed. So far there has
been a discouraging lack of progress made in the carrying out,
which the world expects, of the political decisions which we
reached at the conference particularly those relating to the Polish question. I am frankly puzzled as to why this should be
and must tell you that I do not fully understand in many respects the apparent indifferent attitude of your Government.
Having understood each other so well at Yalta, I am convinced
that the three of us can and will clear away any obstacles
which have developed since then. I intend, therefore, in this
message, to lay before you with complete frankness the problem as I see it.

Although I have in mind primarily the difficulties which
the Polish negotiations have encountered, I must make a brief
mention of our agreement embodied in the Declaration on Lib-

erated Europe. I frankly cannot understand why the recent developments in Rumania should be regarded as not falling within the terms of that Agreement. I hope you will find time personally to examine the correspondence between our Governments on this subject.

However, the part of our agreements at Yalta which has aroused the greatest popular interest and is the most urgent relates to the Polish question. You are aware, of course, that the Commission which we set up has made no progress. I feel this is due to the interpretation which your Government is placing upon the Crimea decisions. In order that there shall be no misunderstanding, I set forth below my interpretations of the points of the Agreement which are pertinent to the difficulties encountered by the Commission in Moscow.

In the discussions that have taken place so far, your Government appears to take the position that the new Polish Provisional Government of National Unity which we agreed should be formed should be little more than a continuation of the present Warsaw Government. I cannot reconcile this either with our agreement or our discussions. While it is true that the Lublin Government is to be reorganized and its members play a prominent role, it is to be done in such a fashion as to bring into being a new government. This point is clearly brought out in several places in the text of the Agreement. I must make it quite plain to you that any such solution which would result in a thinly disguised continuance of the present Warsaw régime would be unacceptable and would cause the people of the United States to regard the Yalta Agreement as having failed.

It is equally apparent that for the same reason the Warsaw Government cannot under the Agreement claim the right to select or reject what Poles are to be brought to Moscow by the Commission for consultation. Can we not agree that it is up to the Commission to select the Polish leaders to come to Moscow to consult in the first instance and invitations be sent out accordingly. If this could be done, I see no great objection to having the Lublin group come first, in order that they may be fully acquainted with the agreed interpretation of the Yalta decisions on this point. It is, of course, understood that if the Lublin group come first, no arrangements would be made independently with them before the arrival of the other Polish leaders called for consultation. In order to facilitate the agreement, the Commission might first of all select a small but representative group of Polish leaders who could suggest other names for the consideration of the Commission. We have not and would not bar or veto any candidate for consultation which Mr. Molotov might propose, being confident that he would not suggest any Poles who would be inimical to the intent of the Crimea decision. I feel that it is not too much to ask that my Ambassador be accorded the same confidence and that any candidate for consultation presented by any one of the Commission be accepted by the others in good faith. It is obvious to me that if the right of the Commission to select these Poles is limited or shared with the Warsaw Government, the very foundation on which our agreement rests would be destroyed.

While the foregoing are the immediate obstacles which, in my opinion, have prevented our Commission from making any progress in this vital matter, there are two other sugges- tions which were not in the agreement but nevertheless have a very important bearing on the result we all seek. Neither of these suggestions has been as yet accepted by your Govern- ment. I refer to:

(1) That there should be the maximum of political tranquil- lity in Poland and that dissident groups should cease any mea- sures and counter-measures against each other. That we should respectively use our influence to that end seems to me eminently reasonable.

(2) It would also seem entirely natural in view of the re- sponsibilities placed upon them by the Agreement that repre- sentatives of the American and British members of the Commission should be permitted to visit Poland. As you will recall, Mr. Molotov himself suggested this at an early meeting of the Commission and only subsequently withdrew it.

I wish I could convey to you how important it is for the successful development of our program of international col- laboration that this Polish question be settled fairly and speed- ily. If this is not done, all of the difficulties and dangers to Allied unity which we had so much in mind in reaching our decisions at the Crimea will face us in an even more acute form. You are, I am sure, aware that the genuine popular support in the United States is required to carry out any gov- ernment policy, foreign or domestic. The American people make up their own mind, and no government action can change it. I mention this fact because the last sentence of your message about Mr. Molotov's attendance at San Francisco made me wonder whether you give full weight to this factor.

From Marshal J. V. Stalin to the President, Mr. Roosevelt (Personal and Most Secret)

I am in receipt of your message on the Berne talks.

You are quite right in saying, with reference to the talks between the Anglo-American and German Commands in Berne or elsewhere, that "the matter now stands in an atmosphere of regrettable apprehension and mistrust."

You affirm that so far no negotiations have been entered into. Apparently you are not fully informed. As regards my military colleagues, they, on the basis of information in their possession, are sure that negotiations did take place and that they ended in an agreement with the Germans, whereby the German Commander on the Western Front, Marshal Kesselring, is to open the front to the Anglo-American troops and let them move east, while the British and Americans have promised, in exchange, to ease the armistice terms for the Germans.

I think that my colleagues are not very far from the truth. If the contrary were the case the exclusion of representatives of the Soviet Command from the Berne talks would be inexplicable.

Nor can I account for the reticence of the British, who have left it to you to carry on a correspondence with me on this unpleasant matter, while they themselves maintain silence, although it is known that the initiative in the matter of the Berne negotiations belongs to the British.

I realize that there are certain advantages resulting to the Anglo-American troops from these separate negotiations in Berne or in some other place, seeing that the AngloAmerican troops are enabled to advance into the heart of Germany almost without resistance; but why conceal this from the Russians, and why were the Russians, their Allies, not forewarned?

And so what we have at the moment is that the Germans on the Western Front have, in fact, ceased the war against Britain and America. At the same time, they continue the war against Russia, the Ally of Britain and the U.S.A.

Clearly this situation cannot help preserve and promote trust between our countries.

I have already written in a previous message, and I think I must repeat, that I and my colleagues would never in any circumstances have taken such a hazardous step, for we realize that a momentary advantage, no matter how great, is overshadowed by the fundamental advantage of preserving and promoting trust between Allies.

A P R I L   3 ,   1 9 4 5

Received on April 5, 1945

Personal and Top Secret
for Marshal Stalin
from President Roosevelt

I have received with astonishment your message of April 3 containing an allegation that arrangements which were made between Field Marshals Alexander and Kesselring at Berne "permitted the Anglo-American troops to advance to the East and the Anglo-Americans promised in return to ease for the Germans the peace terms."

In my previous messages to you in regard to the attempts made in Berne to arrange a conference to discuss a surrender of the German army in Italy I have told you that: (1) No negotiations were held in Berne, (2) The meeting had no political implications whatever, (3) In any surrender of the enemy army in Italy, there would be no violation of our agreed principle of unconditional surrender, (4) Soviet officers would be welcomed at any meeting that might be arranged to discuss surrender.

For the advantage of our common war effort against Germany, which today gives excellent promise of an early success in a disintegration of the German armies, I must continue to assume that you have the same high confidence in my truthfulness and reliability that I have always had in yours.

I have also a full appreciation of the effect your gallant army has had in making possible a crossing of the Rhine by the forces under General Eisenhower and the effect that your forces will have hereafter on the eventual collapse of the German resistance to our combined attacks.

I have complete confidence in General Eisenhower and know that he certainly would inform me before entering into any agreement with the Germans. He is instructed to demand and will demand unconditional surrender of enemy troops that may be defeated on his front. Our advances on the Western Front are due to military action. Their speed has been attributable mainly to the terrific impact of our air power resulting in destruction of German communications, and to the fact that Eisenhower was able to cripple the bulk of the German forces on the Western Front while they were still west of the Rhine.

I am certain that there were no negotiations in Berne at any time, and I feel that your information to that effect must have come from German sources which have made persistent efforts to create dissension between us in order to escape in some measure responsibility for their war crimes. If that was Wolff's purpose in Berne, your message proves that he has had some success.

With a confidence in your belief in my personal reliability and in my determination to bring about, together with you, an unconditional surrender of the Nazis, it is astonishing that a belief seems to have reached the Soviet Government that I have entered into an agreement with the enemy without first obtaining your full agreement.

Finally I would say this; it would be one of the great tragedies of history if, at the very moment of the victory now within our grasp, such distrust, such lack of faith should prejudice the entire undertaking after the colossal losses of life, material and treasure involved.

Frankly, I cannot avoid a feeling of bitter resentment toward your informers, whoever they are, for such vile misrepresentations of my actions or those of my trusted subordinates.

Personal and Secret
from Premier J. V. Stalin
to the President, Mr. F. Roosevelt

I have received your message of April 5.

In my message of April 3, the point was not about integrity
or trustworthiness. I have never doubted your integrity or
trustworthiness, just as I have never questioned the integrity or
trustworthiness of Mr. Churchill. My point is that in the
course of our correspondence a difference of views has arisen
over what an Ally may permit himself with regard to another
and what he may not. We Russians believe that, in view of the
present situation on the fronts, a situation in which the enemy
is faced with inevitable surrender, whenever the representatives of one of the Allies meet the Germans to discuss surrender terms, the representatives of the other Ally should be
enabled to take part in the meeting. That is absolutely necessary, at least when the other Ally seeks participation in the
meeting. The Americans and British, however, have a different opinion: they hold that the Russian point of view is wrong.
For that reason they have denied the Russians the right to be
present at the meeting with the Germans in Switzerland. I
have already written to you, and I see no harm in repeating
that, given a similar situation, the Russians would never have
denied the Americans and British the right to attend such a
meeting. I still consider the Russian point of view to be the
only correct one, because it precludes mutual suspicions and
gives the enemy no chance to sow distrust between us.

2. It is hard to agree that the absence of German resistance
on the Western Front is due solely to the fact that they have
been beaten. The Germans have 147 divisions on the Eastern

Front. They could safely withdraw from 15 to 20 divisions from the Eastern Front to aid their forces on the Western Front. Yet they have not done so, nor are they doing so. They are fighting desperately against the Russians for Zemlenice, an obscure station in Czechoslovakia, which they need just as much as a dead man needs a poultice, but they surrender without any resistance such important towns in the heart of Germany as Osnabrück, Mannheim, and Kassel. You will admit that this behavior on the part of the Germans is more than strange and unaccountable.

3. As regards those who supply my information, I can assure you that they are honest and unassuming people who carry out their duties conscientiously and who have no intention of affronting anybody. They have been tested in action on numerous occasions. Judge for yourself. In February General Marshall made available to the General Staff of the Soviet troops a number of important reports in which he, citing data in his possession, warned the Russians that in March the Germans were planning two serious counter-blows on the Eastern Front; one from Pomerania towards Thorn, the other from the Moravská Ostrava area towards Łódź. It turned out, however, that the main German blow had been prepared and delivered not in the areas mentioned above, but in an entirely different area; namely, in the Lake Balaton area, southwest of Budapest. The Germans, as we now know, had concentrated 35 divisions in the area, 11 of them armored. This, with its great concentration of armor, was one of the heaviest blows of the war, Marshal Tolbukhin succeeded first in warding off disaster and then in smashing the Germans, and was able to do so also because my informants had disclosed—true, with some delay —the plan for the main German blow and immediately apprised Marshal Tolbukhin. Thus I had yet another opportunity to satisfy myself as to the reliability and soundness of my sources of information.

For your guidance in this matter, I enclose a letter sent by Army General Antonov, Chief of Staff of the Red Army, to Major-General Deane.

A P R I L 7 , 1 9 4 5
C o p y .

To Major-General John R. Deane, Head of the Military Mission of the U.S.A. in the U.S.S.R. (Secret)

Dear General Deane,

Please convey to General Marshall the following:

On February 20 I received a message from General Marshall through General Deane, saying that the Germans were forming two groups for a counter-offensive on the Eastern Front: one in Pomerania to strike in the direction of Thorn and the other in the Vienna-Moravská Ostrava area to advance in the direction of Łódź. The southern group was to include the 6th S.S. Panzer Army. On February 12 I received similar information from Colonel Brinkman, head of the Army Section of the British Military Mission.

I am very much obliged and grateful to General Marshall for the information, designed to further our common aims, which he so kindly made available to us.

At the same time, it is my duty to inform General Marshall that the military operations on the Eastern Front in March did not bear out the information furnished by him. For the battles showed that the main group of German troops, which included the 6th S.S. Panzer Army, had been concentrated, not in Pomerania or in the Moravská Ostrava area, but in the Lake Balaton area, whence the Germans launched their offensive in an attempt to break through to the Danube and force it south of Budapest.

Thus, the information supplied by General Marshall was at variance with the actual course of events on the Eastern Front in March.

It may well be that certain sources of this information wanted to bluff both Anglo-American and Soviet Headquarters and divert the attention of the Soviet High Command from the area where the Germans were mounting their main offensive operation on the Eastern Front.

Despite the foregoing, I would ask General Marshall, if possible, to keep me posted with information about the enemy.

I consider it my duty to convey this information to General Marshall solely for the purpose of enabling him to draw the proper conclusions in relation to the source of the information.

Please convey to General Marshall my respect and gratitude.

> *Truly yours,*
> *Army General ANTONOV*
> *Chief of staff of the Red Army*

M A R C H   3 0 ,   1 9 4 5

Personal and Secret
from Premier J. V. Stalin
to the President, Mr. F. Roosevelt

With reference to your message of April 1st, I think I must make the following comments on the Polish question.

The Polish question has indeed reached an impasse.

What is the reason?

The reason is that the U.S. and British Ambassadors in Moscow—members of the Moscow Commission—have departed from the instructions of the Crimea Conference, introducing new elements not provided for by the Crimea Conference.

Namely:

(a) At the Crimea Conference, the three of us regarded the Polish Provisional Government as the government now functioning in Poland and subject to reconstruction, as the government that should be the core of a new Government of National Unity. The U.S. and British Ambassadors in Moscow, however, have departed from that thesis; they ignore the Polish Provisional Government, pay no heed to it, and, at best, place individuals in Poland and London on a par with the Provisional Government. Furthermore, they hold that reconstruction of the Provisional Government should be understood in terms of its abolition and the establishment of an entirely new government. Things have gone so far that Mr. Harriman declared in the Moscow Commission that it might be that not a single member of the Provisional Government would be included in the Polish Government of National Unity.

Obviously, this thesis of the U.S. and British Ambassadors cannot but be strongly resented by the Polish Provisional Government. As regards the Soviet Union, it certainly cannot accept a thesis that is tantamount to direct violation of the Crimea Conference decisions.

(b) At the Crimea Conference, the three of us held that five people should be invited for consultation from Poland and three from London, not more. But the U.S. and British Ambassadors have abandoned that position and insist that each member of the Moscow Commission be entitled to invite an unlimited number from Poland and from London.

Clearly the Soviet Government could not agree to that, because, according to the Crimea decision, invitations should be sent not by individual members of the Commission, but by the Commission as a whole, as a body. The demand for no limit to the number invited for consultation runs counter to what was envisaged at the Crimea Conference.

(c) The Soviet Government proceeds from the assumption that, by virtue of the Crimea decisions, those invited for consultation should be, in the first instance, Polish leaders who recognize the decisions of the Crimea Conference, including the one on the Curzon Line, and, secondly, who actually want friendly relations between Poland and the Soviet Union. The Soviet Government insists on this because the blood of Soviet soldiers, so freely shed in liberating Poland, and the fact that in the past 30 years the territory of Poland has twice been used by an enemy for invading Russia, oblige the Soviet Government to ensure friendly relations between the Soviet Union and Poland.

The U.S. and British Ambassadors in Moscow, however, ignore this and want to invite Polish leaders for consultation regardless of their attitude to the Crimea decisions and to the Soviet Union.

Such, to my mind, are the factors hindering a settlement of the Polish problem through mutual agreement.

In order to break the deadlock and reach an agreed decision, the following steps should, I think, be taken:

(1) Affirm that reconstruction of the Polish Provisional Government implies not its abolition, but its reconstruction by enlarging it, it being understood that the Provisional Government shall form the core of the future Polish Government of National Unity.

(2) Return to the provisions of the Crimea Conference and restrict the number of Polish leaders to be invited to eight persons, of whom five should be from Poland and three from London.

(3) Affirm that the representatives of the Polish Provisional Government shall be consulted in all circumstances, that they be consulted in the first place, since the Provisional Government is much stronger in Poland compared with the individuals to be invited from London and Poland whose influence among the population in no way compares with the tremendous prestige of the Provisional Government.

I draw your attention to this because, to my mind, any other decision on the point might be regarded in Poland as an affront to the people and as an attempt to impose a government without regard to Polish public opinion.

(4) Only those leaders should be summoned for consultation from Poland and from London who recognize the decisions of the Crimea Conference on Poland and who, in practice, want friendly relations between Poland and the Soviet Union.

(5) Reconstruction of the Provisional Government to be

effected by replacing a number of Ministers of the Provisional Government by nominees among the Polish leaders who are not members of the Provisional Government.

As to the ratio of old and new Ministers in the Government of National Unity, it might be established more or less on the same lines as was done in the case of the Yugoslav Government.

I think if these comments are taken into consideration, the Polish question can be settled in a short time.

APRIL 7, 1945

Personal and Secret
from Premier J. V. Stalin
to the Prime Minister,
Mr. W. Churchill

I have received your message of April 1 on the Polish problem. In a relevant message to the President, a copy of which I am also sending to you, I have replied to the salient points about the work of the Moscow Commission on Poland. Concerning the other points in your message, I must say this:

The British and U.S. Ambassadors—members of the Moscow Commission—refuse to consider the opinion of the Polish Provisional Government and insist on inviting Polish leaders for consultation regardless of their attitude to the decisions of the Crimea Conference on Poland or to the Soviet Union. They insist, for example, on Mikolajczyk being invited to Moscow for consultation, and they do so in the form of an ultimatum, ignoring the fact that Mikolajczyk has openly attacked the Crimea Conference decisions on Poland. However, if you deem it necessary, I shall try to induce the Provisional Polish Government to withdraw its objections to inviting Mikolajczyk provided he publicly endorses the decisions of the Crimea Conference on the Polish question and declares in favour of establishing friendly relations between Poland and the Soviet Union.

2. You wonder why the Polish military theatre should be veiled in secrecy. Actually there is no secrecy at all. You forget the circumstance that the Poles regard the despatch of British or other foreign observers to Poland as an affront to their national dignity, especially when it is borne in mind that the Polish Provisional Government feels the British Government has adopted an unfriendly attitude towards it. As to the Soviet Government, it has to take note of the Polish Provisional Government's negative view on sending foreign observers to Poland. Furthermore, you know that, given a different attitude towards it, the Polish Provisional Government would not object to representatives of other countries entering Poland and, as was the case, for example, with representatives of the Czechoslovak Government, the Yugoslav Government and others, would not put any difficulties in their way.

3. I had a pleasant talk with Mrs. Churchill who made a deep impression upon me. She gave me a present from you. Please accept my heartfelt thanks for it.

APRIL 7, 1945

Sent on April 13, 1945

For President Truman

Washington

On behalf of the Soviet Government and on my own behalf, I express to the Government of the United States of America deep regret at the untimely death of President Roosevelt. The American people and the United Nations have lost, in the person of Franklin Roosevelt, a great statesman of world stature and champion of postwar peace and security.

The Government of the Soviet Union expresses its heartfelt sympathy with the American people in their grievous loss and its confidence that the policy of cooperation between the Great Powers who have borne the brunt of the war against the common foe will be promoted in the future as well.

J. STALIN

J. V. Stalin to W. Churchill

I received the joint message from you and President Truman of April 18.

It would appear that you still regard the Polish Provisional Government, not as the core of a future Polish Government of National Unity, but merely as a group on a par with any other group of Poles. It would be hard to reconcile this concept of the position of the Provisional Government and this attitude towards it with the Crimea decision on Poland. At the Crimea Conference the three of us, including President Roosevelt, based ourselves on the assumption that the Polish Provisional Government, as the Government now functioning in Poland and enjoying the trust and support of the majority of the Polish people, should be the core, that is, the main part of a new, reconstructed Polish Government of National Unity.

You apparently disagree with this understanding of the issue. By turning down the Yugoslav example as a model for Poland, you confirm that the Polish Provisional Government cannot be regarded as a basis for, and the core of, a future Government of National Unity.

2. Another circumstance that should be borne in mind is that Poland borders on the Soviet Union, which cannot be said about Great Britain or the U.S.A.

Poland is to the security of the Soviet Union what Belgium and Greece are to the security of Great Britain.

You evidently do not agree that the Soviet Union is entitled to seek in Poland a Government that would be friendly to it, that the Soviet Government cannot agree to the existence in Poland of a Government hostile to it. This is rendered imperative, among other things, by the Soviet people's blood freely shed on the fields of Poland for the liberation of that country. I do not know whether a genuinely representative Government has been established in Greece, or whether the Belgian Government is a genuinely democratic one. The Soviet Union was not consulted when those Governments were being formed, nor did it claim the right to interfere in those matters, because it realises how important Belgium and Greece are to the security of Great Britain.

I cannot understand why in discussing Poland no attempt is made to consider the interests of the Soviet Union in terms of security as well.

3. One cannot but recognise as unusual a situation in which two Governments—those of the United States and Great Britain—reach agreement beforehand on Poland, a country in which the U.S.S.R. is interested first of all and most of all, and, placing its representatives in an intolerable position, try to dictate to it.

I say that this situation cannot contribute to agreed settlement of the Polish problem.

4. I am most grateful to you for kindly communicating the text of Mikolajczyk's declaration concerning Poland's eastern frontier. I am prepared to recommend to the Polish Provisional Government that they take note of this declaration and withdraw their objection to inviting Mikolajczyk for consultation on a Polish Government.

The important thing now is to accept the Yugoslav precedent as a model for Poland. I think that if this is done we shall be able to make progress on the Polish question.

A P R I L 2 4 , 1 9 4 5

Personal and Secret
from Premier J. V. Stalin
to the Prime Minister,
Mr. W. Churchill

I have received your message of April 27 concerning the order of the occupation of Germany and Austria by the Red Army and the Anglo-American armed forces.

For my part I want to tell you that the Soviet Supreme Command has given instructions that whenever Soviet troops contact Allied troops the Soviet Command is immediately to get in touch with the Command of the U.S. or British troops, so that they, by agreement between themselves, (1) establish a temporary tactical demarcation line and (2) take steps to crush within the bounds of their temporary demarcation line all resistance by German troops.

MAY 2, 1945

WAR BOOKS FROM JOVE

08578-2	**AIR WAR SOUTH ATLANTIC** Jeffrey Ethell and Alfred Price	$3.50
08918-4	**BATAAN: THE MARCH OF DEATH** Stanley L. Falk	$3.50
08674-6	**BLOODY WINTER** John M. Waters	$3.95
07294-X	**THE DEVIL'S VIRTUOSOS** David Downing	$2.95
07297-4	**HITLER'S WEREWOLVES** Charles Whiting	$2.95
07134-X	**DAS REICH** Max Hastings	$3.50
08695-9	**THE SECRET OF STALINGRAD** Walter Kerr	$3.50
07427-6	**U-BOAT OFFSHORE** Edwin P. Hoyt	$2.95
08341-0	**THE BATTLE OF THE HUERTGEN FOREST** Charles B. MacDonald	$3.50
08236-8	**WAKE ISLAND** Duane Schultz	$2.95
08887-0	**PATTON'S BEST** Nat Frankel and Larry Smith	$3.50
07393-8	**SIEGFRIED: THE NAZIS' LAST STAND** Charles Whiting	$3.50
09030-1	**A DISTANT CHALLENGE** Edited by Infantry Magazine	$3.50
08054-3	**INFANTRY IN VIETNAM** Albert N. Garland, U.S.A. (ret.)	$3.50
08365-8	**HITLER MUST DIE!** Herbert Molloy Mason, Jr.	$3.95
08810-2	**LITTLE SHIP, BIG WAR: THE SAGA OF DE343** Commander Edward P. Stafford, U.S.N. (ret.)	$3.95
08474-3	**GUADALCANAL** Edwin P. Hoyt	$3.50
08513-8	**PANZER ARMY AFRICA** James Lucas	$3.50
08682-7	**THE END OF THE IMPERIAL JAPANESE NAVY** Masanori Ito	$3.50
07737-2	**48 HOURS TO HAMMELBURG** Charles Whiting	$2.95
07733-X	**THE INCREDIBLE 305th** Wilbur Morrison	$2.95
08066-7	**THE KAMIKAZES** Edwin P. Hoyt	$3.50
07618-X	**KASSERINE PASS** Martin Blumenson	$3.50
08624-X	**THE AMERICAN AIRBORNE INVASION OF NORMANDY** S.L.A. Marshall	$3.95
08732-7	**PORK CHOP HILL** S.L.A. Marshall	$3.50
08940-0	**THE LOS BANOS RAID** Lt. Gen. E.M. Flanagan, Jr.	$3.50
08913-3	**FOUR STARS OF HELL** Laurence Critchell	$3.95
09066-2	**DROP ZONE SICILY** William B. Breuer	$3.50

Dramatic and Revealing
Historical Books From Berkley!

☐ 0-425-09881-8 **THE LAST DAYS OF PATTON** $3.95
Ladislas Farago

☐ 0-425-08480-9 **MONTE CASSINO** $3.95
David Hapgood and David Richardson

☐ 0-425-08481-7 **IVAN THE TERRIBLE** $3.95
Henri Troyat

☐ 0-425-07981-3 **CATHERINE THE GREAT** $4.50
Henri Troyat

☐ 0-425-10495-8 **REFLECTIONS OF THE CIVIL WAR** $3.95
Bruce Catton and John Leekley, eds.

☐ 0-425-07578-8 **THE MURDER OF NAPOLEON** $3.50
Ben Weider and David Hapgood